CAKE

Ladies

CAKE

Ladies

Celebrating a Southern Tradition

Jodi Rhoden

LARK

An Imprint of Sterling Publishing Co., Inc.
New York

WWW.LARKCRAFTS.COM

Senior Editor
NICOLE MCCONVILLE

Editor
BETH SWEET

Creative Director
CHRIS BRYANT

Art Director
TRAVIS MEDFORD

Photographers
LYNNE HARTY
SUSAN PATRICE
JODI RHODEN

Cover Designer
TRAVIS MEDFORD

This book is dedicated to my mother, Sally Elizabeth Brown Rhoden, who first taught me how to cook and how to love, and to all mothers everywhere who show love for their families through the simple daily pleasures of food.

Photo by Blake Madden

Library of Congress Cataloging-in-Publication Data

Rhoden, Jodi.
  Cake ladies : celebrating a Southern tradition / Jodi Rhoden.
-- 1st ed.
    p. cm.
  Includes index.
  ISBN 978-1-60059-789-3 (pb-flexibound : alk. paper)
  1. Cake. 2. Cooking, American--Southern style. I. Title.
  TX771.R485 2011
  641.8'653--dc22
                              2011001868
10 9 8 7 6 5 4 3 2 1

First Edition

Published by Lark Crafts
An Imprint of Sterling Publishing Co., Inc.
387 Park Avenue South, New York, NY 10016

Text © 2011, Jodi Rhoden
Photography © 2011, Lark Crafts, an Imprint of Sterling
Publishing Co., Inc., unless otherwise specified
Illustrations © 2011, Lark Crafts, an Imprint of Sterling
Publishing Co., Inc., unless otherwise specified

Distributed in Canada by Sterling Publishing
c/o Canadian Manda Group, 165 Dufferin Street
Toronto, Ontario, Canada M6K 3H6

Distributed in the United Kingdom by GMC Distribution Services
Castle Place, 166 High Street, Lewes
East Sussex, England BN7 1XU

Distributed in Australia by Capricorn Link (Australia) Pty Ltd.
P.O. Box 704, Windsor, NSW 2756 Australia

If you have questions or comments about this book, please contact:
Lark Crafts
67 Broadway
Asheville, NC 28801
828-253-0467

Manufactured in China

ISBN 13: 978-1-60059-789-3

For information about custom editions, special sales, premium and corporate purchases, please contact Sterling Special Sales Department at 800-805-5489 or specialsales@sterlingpub.com.

For information about desk and examination copies available to college and university professors, requests must be submitted to academic@larkbooks.com. Our complete policy can be found at www.larkcrafts.com.

TABLE OF CONTENTS

INTRODUCTION

Almost every town in the South, large or small, has its cake lady. These are the women who bake the cakes for their community's special occasions: weddings, birthdays, church barbeques, and even funerals. And—as you'll discover when you try the recipes in this book—cake lady cakes are special. Rich pound cakes, delicately iced layer cakes, and towering and fantastical wedding cakes are all part of the profuse and festive outpouring of creativity and sweetness that's characterized Southern baking for generations. It's true that people the world over love and celebrate with cake, but it seems to me that we Southerners enjoy our cakes with a special fervor.

A SHORT HISTORY OF CAKE LADIES

Before electricity and natural gas were common, most women in the South baked their own cakes, often using cast-iron pans in a wood-fired oven. Cake baking was a matter of course for householding women, just another part of cooking. The traditional cakes of the South—caramel cakes, strawberry shortcakes, and pineapple upside-down cakes—come from that era. Often these cakes were made with sweeteners that were cheaper to grow, make, or procure than sugar—ingredients such as sorghum syrup, molasses, and even beets and carrots. Using what was at hand led to the unique recipes and methods known today as Southern cakes.

As technology changed the way people lived, many Southern women started buying instead of baking cakes. Women who found their home-baked cakes in high demand often stepped up to the role of cake lady in the community. For these women, cake making became both a source of secondary income and a way to express their creativity. Then, toward the end of the last century, with the dawn of boxed cake mixes and supermarket cakes, as well as stricter regulations on selling food, the cake lady tradition started to dwindle. People's lives became busier, and food became mass-produced. Many cake ladies retired, and many passed away.

In recent years, there's been a resurgence of interest in the cooking and eating of local foods and in the preservation and revival of regional recipes. Now, a new generation of cake ladies is evolving—bakers, chefs, shop owners, and bloggers all following in the footsteps of their foremothers through hard work, commitment, and delicious cakes. I was inspired to write this book to celebrate these women—both the elders and the newcomers—and to learn about the recipes, the history, and the life experiences these women all share.

MY STORY

Though my mother taught me how to cook as a child in Marietta, Georgia, I came to be a cake lady in a roundabout way through social work and environmental activism. As a social worker in Athens, Georgia, I planted my first garden with teenagers and learned the joy of growing food. I was working at a nonprofit in Boston when I learned to bake artisan breads. I fell in love with baking and devoured all the information I could find on the subject. I began to see baking and gardening as a sustainable means of self-reliance. When I decided to compile a family heirloom cookbook as a wedding gift for my brother and his wife, I rediscovered the recipes and traditions of my native South and connected the dots about not just the food we eat and the food we grow but our common history, as well.

Soon after my son was born, I started baking cakes for friends' weddings, using the recipes I'd collected from my Southern family. I moved on to baking and selling cakes out of my little pink house, and Short Street Cakes was born. I enjoyed the freedom and flexibility of working for myself, and, as a mother, I appreciated the love and care that goes into cooking for a family. I loved, too, the way that cakes marked the seasons and celebrations of people's lives.

It wasn't until my mother mentioned the cake ladies she remembered from her childhood in Monroe, Georgia, that I realized my work as a baker was a part of something larger than myself, a lineage of women who were in similar circumstances and had come to the same conclusions, and met the same challenges and rewards. Their stories fascinated me, so, in addition to expanding my cake business into a retail shop and documenting my experiences on my blog, My Life in Cake, I decided to write a book.

STIRRING IT ALL TOGETHER

I was one year into running my own cake shop, two years into writing a blog about cake, three years into being a cake lady, and four years into being a mom, when I was given the opportunity to write this book. By the next summer, I was travelling the back roads of the South, in search of cakes and cake ladies with a story to tell. Some of the women I set out to interview were already my friends or mentors, like Elyse Manning and Lisa Goldstein. Some came to me through word-of-mouth, their skills in baking known far and wide. And some seemed to appear through divine intervention, like when I got lost and ended up at Matilda Reed's diner in the mountains of North Carolina, or when I inquired about cake ladies in the Pine Apple Grocery in Alabama.

"As I listened to the cake ladies tell of their struggles and their joys, I found over and over that it is love, first and foremost, that motivates them, and that love is the one essential ingredient to baking beautiful and delicious cakes."

I'm so grateful to have met each of the women in these pages. I'm grateful they chose to share their stories and their recipes with me, and I'm grateful to have the opportunity to share them with you. I was welcomed so graciously into these women's lives, their farms, their shops, and their kitchens. I baked with many new and old friends, looked at family photo albums, and shared laughter and cake with them. As I listened to the cake ladies tell of their struggles and their joys, I found over and over that it is love, first and foremost, that motivates them, and that love is the one essential ingredient to baking beautiful and delicious cakes.

This book is a celebration of that love. It's a celebration of the value of hard work, and the redemptive power of creating something beautiful with your own hands. It's also a celebration of the South—not the South of antebellum homes and high tea, but the South of the

"A new generation of cake ladies is evolving—bakers, chefs, shop owners, and bloggers all following in the footsteps of their foremothers through hard work, commitment, and delicious cakes."

real people who live here: hurricane survivors and school bus drivers and Latina immigrants and Cherokee grandmothers. It's a celebration of this lush, beautiful, and often wild landscape in which I am blessed to live: kudzu and apple orchards and bayous and barns and cropland, as well as sprawling cities and gleaming highways. It's a celebration of Southern food—those recipes and methods that are unique to the South's climate and culture, beloved as our common heritage beyond race and class. But most of all, this book is a celebration of Southern cakes and the women who bake them.

BAKING BASICS

BAKING CAKES FROM SCRATCH: INGREDIENTS, TOOLS, AND TIPS

A cake lady will tell you that baking and decorating a beautiful cake from scratch brings a wonderful sense of pride and accomplishment, but it also takes a bit of practice. Successful cake baking involves understanding the ingredients and tools required, a willingness to follow recipes closely (without substitutions or omissions), and careful attention to the process.

Most cakes are made up of seven basic elements in different combinations: fats, sugars, eggs, liquid ingredients, flour, leavening, and flavorings. The goal in incorporating these elements together into a cake batter is to create as much lightness, softness, and moistness as possible. The key to achieving this is knowing each ingredient well, understanding how each ingredient behaves under certain conditions, and using the correct baking tools and equipment.

THE ANATOMY OF A CAKE

❧ INGREDIENTS ❧

Fats

BUTTER: Pure butter lends rich flavor and moisture to cake, and, when creamed well with sugar, creates a structure on which to build the rest of the batter. Salted or unsalted is a matter of preference where not otherwise stated. I always bake with salted butter, because I find that the extra salt enhances the flavors of the cake. Unless otherwise directed, butter should always be softened to room temperature before creaming with sugars.

VEGETABLE SHORTENING: Vegetable shortening is vegetable oil that has been chemically altered to be solid at room temperature, like butter or lard. Shortening is useful in that it stabilizes (prevents from melting or breaking down) batters and icings, but I prefer to bake with pure butter.

OIL: Pure vegetable oil is the base for many rich cakes with fruit, such as hummingbird cake, some carrot cakes, and many apple cakes. Canola, soybean, or peanut oil all work well in cakes; olive oil, because of its strong flavor and low burning temperature, does not.

LARD: Pig fat, or lard, has long been a staple of Southern baking. Once an economical alternative to butter or vegetable oil, lard has been replaced with vegetable shortening in recent decades, owing to the decline of small-scale homestead hog farming, and concerns over lard's high concentration of saturated fats. While many bakers steer clear of lard, others are rediscovering its superior results in pastries such as piecrust and biscuit dough, while also recognizing that highly processed, hydrogenated vegetable shortening may pose its own health risks. Unsalted butter can be substituted where lard is called for; oil cannot.

Sugars

WHITE SUGAR: White sugar is made by refining tropical sugarcane into dry crystals. Although Southern bakers have used a variety of sweeteners in their cakes, white sugar remains the preferred choice for achieving great results. White sugar "conditions" a batter, lending it softness, and the caramelizing of the sugars on the surface of a cake's layers (known as "browning") is part of what makes cake delicious.

MOLASSES: The syrupy by-product of refining sugar, molasses has a higher nutritional content than sugar.

BROWN SUGAR: Brown sugar is made by adding some molasses back into the white sugar; it is a moist sugar with a deeper, caramel flavor.

SORGHUM MOLASSES: This is a sweet syrup made from sorghum cane, commonly grown in the South before World War II. Sorghum was brought to the South in the 17th century by African slaves, and was, at one time, the most widely available sweetener for cakes in the South.

Eggs

Eggs contain both protein (in the white) and fats (in the yolk, sometimes called the yellow). The protein in egg whites allows air to be trapped in the batter, so eggs act as a leavening agent as well as lending rich flavor and texture to cakes.

In recipes that call for separated eggs, take care not to let any of the yolk break into the white, as the presence of any fat will inhibit the whites from whipping to their full volume.

Eggs should always be at room temperature before use in a cake. Warmer eggs allow more air to be incorporated into the batter during mixing, resulting in lighter cakes. If you forget to take your eggs out of the refrigerator ahead of time, place cold, uncracked eggs in a bowl of hot tap water for five minutes to bring them to room temperature.

To avoid getting eggshells into your batter, crack the eggs into a separate bowl before adding them to the batter. If small pieces of eggshell go into the bowl, use half of a cracked eggshell to fish it out; it's almost impossible to grab a broken eggshell fragment with your fingers.

Cakes that omit the yolks are called "white cakes," recipes that include yolks are called "yellow cakes."

Liquid Ingredients

A variety of milks and juices can be used for the liquid portion of a cake recipe. Buttermilk, sour cream, coconut milk, and pineapple juice are all examples of liquids that are used to add moisture and flavor and to activate the flour and leavening in a cake batter.

Flour

Refined white flour, from the wheat plant, is unique among grains due to its gluten content. Gluten is the protein that traps air bubbles in batters and breads. As cake or bread is baked, the air bubbles created by the leavening heat up and expand, and the gluten stretches with it, causing the cake to rise. Though gluten-free baking has become popular in recent years, I appreciate gluten—the gluten in flour is what has enabled bakers to create beautiful breads, cakes, and pies over the centuries, and has allowed baking to become such a refined and celebrated art. The flour used in Southern cakes is unique to the region since the wheat that grows well in the South tends to have a lower protein content, lending itself to lighter, softer cakes and biscuits.

All-purpose and self-rising flours are forms of white flour, flour that has had the wheat bran and wheat germ removed. Whole wheat flour is milled with the bran and germ included, which makes it more dense both in texture and in nutrients.

When flour comes into contact with liquid, the gluten proteins begin to stretch and elongate. Care must be taken when baking cakes to mix the batter enough to fully activate the gluten so the cake will rise, while not overbeating the batter (thus overdeveloping the gluten) and making the cake tough and chewy.

Leavening

While good creaming incorporates air into the batter, and eggs and flour hold the air bubbles in the cake to make it rise, mineral leaveners such as baking soda and baking powder create even more air to create a lighter cake. Leavening agents became popular in the 1800s, opening the doors for a much wider range of baking options.

BAKING SODA is, essentially, a form of salt: sodium bicarbonate. It reacts with acid (such as buttermilk, sour cream, or vinegar) to release carbon dioxide, which helps the cake rise.

BAKING POWDER is a blend of baking soda and other acid salts, most often cream of tartar and bulking agents such as potato starch. For this reason, baking soda and baking powder are called for in differing amounts in recipes and are not interchangeable.

To take advantage of the immediate chemical reaction of the leavening in the batter, bake your batter immediately upon incorporating the final ingredients.

Flavorings

VANILLA AND OTHER EXTRACTS: Extracts are used to enhance flavor. Vanilla, a warm, scented extract of the seedpod of an orchid, is the most commonly used flavoring extract in cakes.

SALT: Salt enhances flavor, strengthens gluten, prevents spoilage, and aids in the leavening process.

SPICES: Spices such as cinnamon, clove, nutmeg, and ginger are used to enhance the flavor of a cake. Like salt, these ingredients should be sifted into the batter with the dry ingredients.

FRUITS AND NUTS: Adding fruits and nuts is possibly the most satisfying and creative aspect of cake baking. Folding coconut, pecans, pineapple, strawberries, carrots, raisins, and other sweet foods into cake batter lends flavor, texture, and depth to a simple cake.

TOOLS OF THE TRADE

STAND MIXERS: A stand mixer is an electric mixer mounted on a stand, allowing for hands-free mixing. A heavy-duty stand mixer can be expensive, but a good one can last a lifetime.

HAND MIXERS: A hand mixer is a lighter-duty version of the stand mixer. The baker has to hold the mixer in the bowl to incorporate the ingredients.

ATTACHMENTS: The paddle attachment is used for creaming and mixing in stand mixers. A whisk attachment is a wire, balloon-shaped whisk used for whipping egg whites. Beaters are the all-purpose attachments for handheld mixers.

SIFTER: A sifter uses a mesh screen to separate lumps in dry ingredients, incorporate leavening and spices evenly, and lighten flour for a cake batter.

SPATULAS: Two kinds of spatulas are used in cake baking: rubber spatulas and offset spatulas. Rubber spatulas are flexible and are used in the mixing of batters and icings. An offset spatula has a rigid metal surface that's ideal for spreading icings.

DOUBLE BOILER: A double boiler is a set of two nesting saucepans. The bottom saucepan contains simmering water, while the top contains the sauce, custard, or icing that is cooking. Double boilers allow for gentler cooking of delicate icings and fillings.

PASTRY CUTTER: A pastry cutter (also called a pastry blender) cuts cold fats into flour for shortcake, biscuits, and pie dough.

CAKE PANS: Metal pans for baking come in all shapes and sizes. Generally, a heavier pan will allow for more even heat distribution, allowing for more consistent and even baking.

OVEN: The oven is the most essential part of cake baking—an even, all-over heat is what transforms a lowly batter into a lovely cake! Most cakes bake best between 325°F and 375°F, but ovens can vary. To avoid uneven baking (many ovens have "hot spots" where the temperature is higher), rotate cakes in the oven at least once during the early part of the baking process.

You'll find Kitchen Wisdom tips from the cake ladies sprinkled among the various recipes in this book. But here are some tips concerning the question I get asked the most about baking a cake.

HOW DO YOU TELL WHEN IT'S DONE? This is possibly the hardest part of baking a cake. If you remove the cake too early, the center will be gooey, and the cake could fall. If you bake it for too long, it can become hard and dry. Further complicating matters, baking times in recipes are not exact, as they are affected by factors such as variations in oven temperature, the presence of other items in the same oven—even the weather and humidity can affect baking times. The following are the most commonly used methods to determine when a cake is done:

THE TOOTHPICK TEST: Stick a wooden toothpick in the center of the cake. If the toothpick comes out clean and no batter sticks to it, the cake is done.

THE CAKE WILL PULL FROM THE SIDES OF THE PAN: As moisture escapes from the cake during baking, and the eggs and flour set, the cake will shrink towards the center, and the sides of the cake will pull away from the sides of the pan.

COLOR: While the color of a done cake can vary depending on the ingredients, most cakes have a golden, honey-colored hue on the top crust when fully baked.

SMELL: I believe that the best indicator of cake doneness (and hardest baking skill to perfect) is smell. There's a moment during baking when the "done smell" hits your nose, and you know, at that moment, that the cake is perfectly baked, and you can remove it from the oven. The smell is indescribable, but once you learn it, the smell method will never fail.

Good luck and happy baking!

Jodi R.

Jodi's Kitchen Wisdom

Most any cake recipe can be used for cupcakes; a batch of cake batter typically makes two to three dozen standard-sized cupcakes. Line muffin tins with cupcake papers, then fill the cups two-thirds full. You'll also need to reduce the baking time by about 10 minutes.

CAKE
Ladies

The creativity and wisdom of these extraordinary women extend beyond kitchen walls into the lives they lead and the communities they love. Get to know them, share in their stories, and indulge in some of their most prized cake recipes.

Betty Compton

Cedar Grove, North Carolina

WHO YOU ARE IS WHO YOU LOVE

When Betty Compton returns home from work to her farm in Cedar Grove, North Carolina, she often "puts together" a pound cake, something she's done for 45 years. Like many Southern women, Betty always has a pound cake on her kitchen counter. Her cakes are in high demand from family members, friends, and her church community in Cedar Grove, but she claims the only thing that's special about them is the pan she bakes them in. Fifteen years ago, Betty was in Asheville, North Carolina, for the weekend and found a vintage tube pan for 50 cents in an antique store.

"Fifty cents, I paid for that pan," says Betty. "I came home and I kept looking at this thing, thinking, wonder what it would be like to bake a cake in this pan! So I put a pound cake in it—oh, my gosh, did it change that

cake! It's the very same recipe, but it takes on a texture. Really, truly, there are people who have offered me 500 dollars for this pan. But never have I ever found another pan like this one."

Born a sharecropper's daughter in rural Nash County, North Carolina, just east of the small town of Zebulon, Betty credits her rich life story and achievements to luck. In high school, she finished first in the school bus driving competition at the rodeo and used her winnings to pay for nursing school. She went on to graduate with the first class of nurse practitioners in North Carolina, become a tenured professor at the University

"Who you are is about who you love, not about whether somebody loves you."

of North Carolina School of Medicine, and travel the world training rural midwives. The former tobacco farm where Betty lives in Cedar Grove has been in her husband Dwight's family since the 1700s. Dwight and their sons began a sod grass farming business there a little over a decade ago.

As I watched Betty put together a pound cake, while she made lunch for her family and our friend David played fiddle in her kitchen, she spoke of how baking her famous pound cakes connects her to her community. "Dwight's mother is the one who taught me how to bake, but I got the recipe from a woman named Ruth Pope. Ruth Pope was the master baker around here, so I would go and stand by her side while she was baking, canning, and freezing, and I learned all those skills." But Betty says that the most important thing she learned is that baking is an essential way for her to give. "If you are in a community, one of the ways that you give back is that you take food to the home. If there's a death in a family, you are part of the group of people that wraps that family in love and care. You know you're bringing the pound cake. You know somebody else will bring their wonderful chicken casserole. You know each other's gifts—you wrap around each other's gifts. That is a special thing about living in a community."

When I asked Betty what motivates her to share so much with others, from food, to healing, to mothering, she said, "I think my mother, as much as anybody, impressed upon me that who you are is about who you love, not about whether somebody loves you, and it's the ones who are a little bit harder to love that matter. What God's given us, we don't get to keep it. We've got to send it on. But if you give, it comes back to you in so many ways."

Bless Those Eggs: Buying Local and Putting By

Growing food for her family, "putting by" (canning and freezing), and buying and eating local food isn't some new trend for Betty but a way of life that goes back for generations. Betty puts by 100 quarts of green beans, 30 quarts of baby limas, 20 quarts of corn, and 60 quarts of tomatoes from her garden every year. She also makes jams, jellies, and pickles from her crops. "I just like to keep my friends in jellies and jams," she says. "It doesn't feel like work to me. It grounds me." Betty buys all of her eggs from the Latta Brothers Egg Ranch in nearby Hillsborough, North Carolina. Latta Brothers eggs are the only ones sold at the Efland Supermarket between Hillsborough and Cedar Grove, but Betty likes to go directly to the farm each week to get the eggs for her pound cakes. She says, "Mr. Latta died recently at 82. When we'd get eggs, he'd say, 'Is Ms. Betty making her pound cake?' Dwight would say, 'Oh, yes, these are her eggs.' And there might be five or six that he's sure that I'm going to use—he kind of blesses them. He used to bless those eggs."

Betty's Kitchen Wisdom

Betty shared a couple of the tips she learned from her baking mentor, Ruth Pope:

When you're adding the flour and milk to a cake, you have to alternate—start with the flour and end with the flour.

Don't ever open the oven while the cake is baking—wait until the cake is done.

Vanilla Almond Pound Cake

Pound cake may be the single most popular cake among Southern bakers. Like many Southern favorites, the recipe is simple and calls for readily available ingredients. British in origin, pound cake was so named because it traditionally contained one pound each of butter, sugar, flour, and eggs. Baked at a low temperature in a tube, loaf-shaped or bundt pan, a pound cake is rarely decorated (other than the occasional simple glaze) and can be eaten hot out of the oven at room temperature, or sliced, toasted, and buttered. Myriad versions of this cake have evolved over time, but Ms. Betty's is a great example of a simple, classic pound cake recipe that lends itself to an array of flavorings and variations.

PREP TIME: 20 to 25 minutes
BAKING TIME: 1 hour, 20 minutes
COOLING TIME: at least 1 hour before cutting

YOU WILL NEED

2 sticks (1 cup) unsalted butter, softened
½ cup vegetable shortening
3 cups sugar
5 large eggs, at room temperature
3 cups all-purpose flour
½ teaspoon baking powder
1 cup whole milk, at room temperature
1 teaspoon pure vanilla extract
½ teaspoon pure almond extract

Position a rack in the lower third of the oven and preheat the oven to 300°F.

PREPARE THE PAN

Spray a 10 x 6-inch tube pan liberally with nonstick cooking spray, or, using your fingers, coat the inside walls and bottom of the pan with butter.

MIX THE BATTER

Add the butter and the shortening to the bowl of a stand mixer fitted with a paddle attachment, and beat on low speed until fully combined. Stop the mixer and use a rubber spatula to scrape down the paddle, bottom, and sides of the bowl.

Add the sugar, 1 cup at a time, beating at a low speed after each addition. Beat on low speed for 3 to 5 minutes or until the mixture is light and fluffy. Stop the mixer twice during mixing, and scrape down the paddle, bottom, and sides of the bowl. Add the eggs to the mixture one at a time, stopping the mixer and scraping down the bowl after each addition. Beat the eggs into the creamed mixture for 5 minutes or until they are fully incorporated and the entire mixture is light in color and texture.

Add the flour and the baking powder to a sifter over a separate, clean bowl. Sift the flour and baking powder together, and set aside.

Add the vanilla and almond extract to the milk. Add 1 cup of the dry ingredients mixture to the creamed mixture and beat on low speed until just incorporated. Add ½ cup of the milk and extract mixture, and beat on low speed until it is just incorporated. Continue to alternate adding the dry mixture and milk mixture to the creamed mixture, ending with flour. Stop the mixer and thoroughly scrape down the paddle, bottom, and sides of the bowl, then continue to beat the mixture on low speed for 1 minute or until all the ingredients are fully incorporated and the cake batter is light and uniform in color and texture. Be careful not to beat the mixture once the ingredients are all smoothly incorporated, however, as this will toughen the batter and create air tunnels in the finished cake.

BAKE THE CAKE

Gently scrape the batter into the greased tube pan. Smooth the top with a spatula and shake the pan slightly to settle the batter into the edges of the pan. Place in the preheated oven, and bake for 1 hour and 20 minutes, or until the top crust of the cake is a deep, golden brown, the surface springs back when touched with your finger, and the sides of the cake have pulled away from the sides of the pan. Allow the cake to cool at least one hour in the pan. To remove the cake from the pan, place a large heat-proof plate on the top of the tube pan. Wearing oven mitts, grasp both sides of the pan and plate firmly, and quickly invert the pan onto the plate. Remove the pan, leaving the cake to cool on the plate.

Once the cake is cooled, it should be stored covered, at room temperature. Pound cakes often improve in flavor over the course of a few days and will keep at room temperature for up to a week.

Berry Sauce and Fresh Whipped Cream

Pound cake combines beautifully with fruit sauces and fresh whipped cream.

Berry Sauce

2 pints fresh berries
½ cup sugar

Add berries (Betty uses blackberries from her garden, but raspberries or wine berries are also fine choices) and sugar to a bowl, and mash with a fork until the sugar dissolves. Spoon the berry sauce over slices of pound cake and top with fresh whipped cream.

Fresh Whipped Cream

1 cup heavy whipping cream
¼ cup sugar

Combine whipping cream and sugar in the bowl of a stand mixer. Using the whisk attachment, whisk at the highest speed for 1 to 2 minutes or until the cream becomes stiff and smooth.

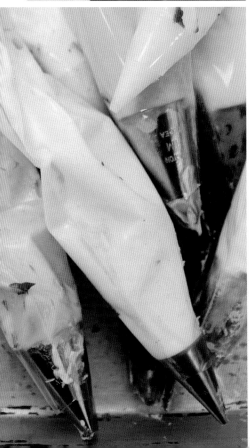

Johnnie Gabriel

Marietta, Georgia

PRETTY IS AS PRETTY DOES

I do identify as a cake lady, but, even more, I identify as a business lady in the community." Johnnie Gabriel and I are sharing a corner table at Gabriel's Desserts, in a strip mall a few blocks off of the town square in Marietta, Georgia. As she answers questions from employees, takes phone calls, and greets customers, Johnnie describes how she became Marietta's cake lady. When a recession in the late 1980s hurt her husband's business, Johnnie began baking cakes out of her home to make ends meet. On finding out that Mary Moon, Marietta's preeminent cake lady at the time, was planning to retire, she asked if she could buy her recipes. "Well, not only did she give me her recipes, but she gave me her clients as well!" That little home-based business eventually grew to be Gabriel's Desserts, Johnnie's busy, award-winning cake shop and restaurant in my hometown of Marietta, Georgia.

Growing up in Macon, Georgia, Johnnie says, "My family wouldn't dare put a store-bought cake on the table. My grandmother always baked cakes. I'd hang on the side of the table while she baked, and I got to lick the bowl. I got my innate ability to bake from her." She also learned the value of a strong work ethic from the women in her family. "I come from a long line of women who made it happen, and they usually made it happen for their children. The women in my family scrambled to provide for their children, and get their own education. They baked their own cakes and cleaned their own houses, even though both my mother and my grandmother worked outside of the home. You did what you had to do, but you had a meal on the table every night, everybody's feet were under that table, and you had one meal together. We were encouraged to be good people, and to work hard. My grandmother and my mother always said, 'pretty is as pretty does.' That doesn't mean you can't speak your mind and speak the truth. I realize now that I am older that it is probably prettier to speak your mind before you are mad, and speak the truth while you can still say it without a lot of emotion.

"Growing up, we didn't know what a cake lady was, because we baked all of our own cakes," says Johnnie. But she understands now the joy that comes with a role that fulfills a need in the community. "It's such a pleasure when an 18-year-old comes in and says, 'Ms. Johnnie, you made my first birthday cake, and it was a fresh strawberry cake.' It makes you feel so proud. People have great and warm memories about cakes, and I just appreciate being able to be a part of it."

> " People have great and warm memories about cakes, and I just appreciate being able to be a part of it."

While she still loves making cakes, Johnnie says that "Baking is more a business for me now. But the beautiful part is that this business provides 42 families with a check every Friday. When I find myself thinking, 'where's the love?' I remember that it's a living for 42 families. We have single mothers here, and three or four ladies who have come through drug court, and they've done all the work and they are so excited to have a job. So yes, it is now business. It's not that I'm just baking a whole bowl full of love and giving it away, but it's a resource for the community, and there's love in that. And all these people love each other. When someone's gotta have a tooth pulled, we're going to take care of that, and they are going to pay us back 10 dollars a week. We aren't high end, we aren't a chain—we are a local business from scratch. So that's where the love comes in for me."

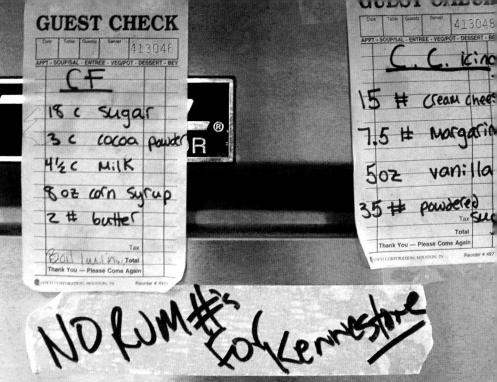

GUEST CHECK

GUEST CHECK

413048

APPT · SOUP/SAL · ENTREE · VEG/POT · DESSERT · BEV

CF

18 c	sugar	
3 c	cocoa powder	
4½ c	Milk	
8 oz	corn syrup	
2 #	butter	

Tax

Boil ~~~~ Total

Thank You — Please Come Again

413048

APPT · SOUP/SAL · ENTREE · VEG/POT · DESSERT · BE

C. C. icing

15 #	cream chees	
7.5 #	margarin	
5 oz	vanilla	
35 #	powdered sug	

Tax

Total

Thank You — Please Come Again

NO RUM #'s FOR Kennestone

Lemon Cheese Layer Cake

Lemon cheese cake is a traditional Southern layer cake, which, despite its name, contains no cheese. It also bears no relation to cheesecake, the classic custard-based cake so common in the Northeastern United States. Lemon cheese is the traditional Southern name for what the wider culinary world calls lemon curd: a translucent, cooked filling made with lemons, butter, sugar, and egg yolks. A classic Southern lemon cheese cake is a basic yellow layer cake iced on the top, sides, and between the layers with the lemon cheese.

PREP TIME: 30 minutes (lemon cheese only)
COOLING TIME: 1½ to 2 hours
DECORATING TIME: 10 minutes

YOU WILL NEED

- 3 freshly baked, cooled 9-inch layers of Yellow Layer Cake (see page 39)
- 3 fresh lemons
- 6 egg yolks
- 1 cup sugar
- 2 sticks (1 cup) unsalted butter

PREPARE THE LEMONS

Use a handheld citrus zester to remove just the outermost yellow rind (the zest) from the 3 lemons. Slice and juice the lemons, straining out any seeds or pulp and retaining the juice.

Fill the bottom of a double boiler one-third of the way full with water, and bring to a boil on medium heat on the stovetop. Place the juice and zest in the top of the double boiler, along with all the remaining ingredients, and set over the boiling water. Stir frequently while cooking until the mixture is thick enough for a thick layer to cling to the spoon, 15 to 25 minutes. Transfer the lemon cheese to a clean bowl and set aside, covered, until cooled completely to room temperature, about 1½ hours. Stir it intermittently (every 10 or 15 minutes) while it cools to prevent it from forming a "skin" on the surface. Once cool, the lemon cheese should be very thick. If not, refrigerate until thick enough to spread.

ASSEMBLE THE CAKE

Trim any uneven areas from the top of the cake layers with a serrated knife to create a level surface on each. Invert the first layer onto a cake plate, parchment side up. Carefully peel the parchment off the cake and throw it away. Spread about ½ cup of the lemon cheese on the top of the cake with an offset spatula, pushing it to the edges of the layer so that it begins to drip down the sides. Place the second cake layer on top of the first and repeat the process of removing the parchment paper and spreading the lemon cheese. Repeat with the third layer, and then cover the sides with the lemon cheese. When all the lemon cheese has been used and the top and sides of the cake are covered, leave the cake in place at room temperature for several hours to set. When the lemon cheese is firm, the cake is ready to serve. The cake will keep, covered and refrigerated, for up to a week.

Johnnie's Kitchen Wisdom

Lemon cheese can be refrigerated for up to two weeks or frozen for up to six months.

For a deluxe variation on an already beautiful and flavorful cake, you can ice the cake with Seven-Minute Icing (page 43) once the lemon curd has fully set. Johnnie says, "We grew up in Macon and Albany eating lemon cheese cake. When I came to Marietta, I found out that people want an icing on that cake, so you've got to let your lemon cheese set, and then put the Seven-Minute Icing on that, and that is to die for. I love the lemon cheese—that's my favorite and that was my family's favorite."

Caramel Cake

Nearly all the cake ladies I've met mention Caramel Cake as a family favorite. This cake is truly a labor of love, as cooking the caramel is a time-consuming task and can be frustrating on your first try. But, like riding a bike, once you get a feel for it, you'll get it right every time. I've used many different recipes for cooked caramel icing, but I've found Johnnie's to be the most reliable and simple.

PREP TIME: 20 minutes
BAKING TIME: about 25 minutes
COOLING TIME: about 1 hour
ICING PREP TIME: 25 minutes (icing only)
DECORATING TIME: 10 minutes

YOU WILL NEED
FOR THE CAKE:

- 3 freshly baked, cooled, and trimmed 9-inch layers of Yellow Layer Cake (page 39)

FOR THE ICING:

- 3 cups sugar, divided
- ¾ cup evaporated milk
- 1½ sticks (¾ cup) salted butter
- 1 tablespoon white corn syrup
- 1 teaspoon pure vanilla extract

NOTE: A candy thermometer will make cooking the caramel much easier; if you don't own one, see No Candy Thermometer? (page 38).

MAKE THE ICING

Have all your ingredients measured and ready. Place ½ cup of the sugar in a heavy-bottomed saucepan over medium heat. As the sugar begins melting, gently shake the pan to keep it spread evenly over the bottom but not on the sides. The sugar will melt and begin to brown. Stir gently with a wooden spoon, so the sugar browns evenly.

When the sugar is "a little lighter than the skin of an almond" in color, begin to pour in the evaporated milk slowly while stirring vigorously. The mixture will begin to boil furiously and the sugar will start to seize up. Continue to stir the mixture to break up the chunks of sugar. Once all the milk is added and combined with the caramelized sugar, quickly add the remaining sugar, butter, and corn syrup, stirring to mix well. Attach a candy thermometer to the side of the saucepan and allow the mixture to come to a boil. Stir intermittently to make sure that no chunks of sugar are burning on the bottom of the pan. If you do see signs of burning, turn the heat down a little, stir, and allow the mixture to continue to boil. Boil on medium heat for 10 to 20 minutes, until the candy thermometer reads exactly 248°F.

When the mixture has reached 248°F, remove the saucepan from the heat, and very carefully transfer the mixture into the clean, dry bowl of a stand mixer fitted with the paddle attachment. With the motor running on low, add the vanilla; stand back—it can splatter. Beat the mixture on medium speed until it begins to cool, lose its gloss, and thickens but is still pourable. Avoid splashing or spilling the caramel on yourself at all times—it is extremely hot and burns instantly.

ASSEMBLE THE CAKE

Invert the first layer of the cake onto a cake plate, parchment side up. Carefully peel the parchment off and throw it away. Working very quickly, pour or spoon about ½ cup of the caramel on the top surface of the cake. Use an offset spatula to push the caramel to the edges of the layer so that it begins to drip down the sides. Place the second cake layer on top of the first and repeat the process, removing the parchment paper and spreading the caramel. Repeat with the third layer, and then cover the sides with the remaining caramel. The caramel will set into a soft, somewhat grainy icing. This icing does not have to be pretty—your goal is to get all the caramel on the cake before it hardens, not to create perfectly smooth lines. Drips or a slightly inconsistent appearance is perfectly okay with this iced cake.

Caramel Cake is special because of the time and care it takes to make it right, and it has a rustic appeal all its own. If the caramel icing gets too firm to spread over the cake and top layer, scrape it into a clean, small saucepan and heat over medium low, stirring constantly with a wooden spoon, until it liquefies again. Stir it well to cool briefly, then finish icing the cake.

No Candy Thermometer?

If you don't have a candy thermometer, use this tried-and-true cold water candy test to determine when your caramel has reached 248°F (the desired "firm ball" stage). As your caramel is cooking, occasionally spoon a drop or two of the boiling mixture into ice water. If it dissipates, keep cooking. If it forms a soft, gooey ball that doesn't hold its shape, you've reached about 240°F, or "soft ball" stage, and you need to keep cooking. You'll know you've reached 248°F when the caramel dropped into the ice water forms a firm ball that holds its shape but flattens when squeezed. Now the caramel is ready to be removed from the heat and beaten in the mixer. Be careful not to overcook the caramel. You'll know you have if it turns to hard candy when dropped into the ice water.

Safety Tip

When cooking caramel, it's a good idea to work with a bowl of ice water nearby. If you are accidentally burned by the hot syrup, submerge your skin immediately in the cold water.

Johnnie's Kitchen Wisdom

Most cake ladies use a cast-iron skillet to cook caramel. Johnnie opts for a heavy-bottomed stainless steel saucepan instead because its depth makes stirring easier and prevents burns.

Yellow Layer Cake

This recipe for Yellow Layer Cake provides the base for so many wonderful recipes— Johnnie's Lemon Cheese Layer Cake and her Caramel Cake both use this Yellow Layer Cake for the layers. It is also excellent with any kind of chocolate icing you like!

PREP TIME: 20 minutes
BAKING TIME: about 25 minutes
COOLING TIME: about 1 hour

YOU WILL NEED

- 1 stick (½ cup) unsalted butter, softened
- ½ cup vegetable shortening
- 2 cups sugar
- 4 large eggs, separated and at room temperature
- 3 cups all-purpose flour
- 2 teaspoons baking powder
- ½ teaspoon salt
- ½ cup whole milk, at room temperature
- ½ cup buttermilk, at room temperature
- ¼ cup heavy cream, at room temperature
- 1 tablespoon pure vanilla extract

PREPARE THE PANS

Spray the bottom and sides of three 9-inch round cake pans liberally with vegetable oil cooking spray. Place your pans on a sheet of parchment paper and trace three circles the same size as the bottom of the pans. Cut the circles out and place in the bottom of the greased pans.

MIX THE BATTER

Beat the butter, shortening, and sugar together in the bowl of a stand mixer fitted with the paddle attachment until light and fluffy, stopping the mixer twice during mixing, and scraping down the paddle, bottom, and sides of the bowl. Add the egg yolks to the mixture one at a time, stopping the mixer and scraping down the bowl after each addition. Beat the egg yolks into the creamed mixture for 5 minutes, or until they are fully incorporated and the entire mixture is light in color and texture.

Sift the flour, baking powder, and salt into a separate bowl and set aside. In another bowl, combine the milk, buttermilk, cream, and vanilla.

Combine the dry and wet ingredients with the creamed mixture: With the blender on low speed, alternately add the dry ingredients and the wet ingredients to the creamed mixture in four parts, beginning and ending with the dry ingredients and scraping down the bowl between additions. Blend just until the ingredients are fully incorporated.

Using the whisk attachment on the stand mixer, whip the egg whites in a clean bowl until they hold a stiff peak. Use a spatula to gently fold the whipped egg whites into the cake batter in three parts.

BAKE THE CAKE

Gently scrape the batter into the three pans, dividing the batter evenly between the pans. Place in the preheated oven and bake for 22 to 26 minutes, or until a knife inserted into the center of the cake comes out clean and the sides of the cake have pulled away from the sides of the pan. Allow the cakes to cool for 20 minutes before removing the layers from the pans and setting on a wire rack to finish cooling.

Johnnie's Kitchen Wisdom

If you don't have buttermilk in your refrigerator, improvise by measuring 1½ teaspoons of white or apple cider vinegar into your measuring cup and then adding enough whole milk to equal ½ cup. Let the mixture sit for a minute or two, and the vinegar will curdle the milk to create the same flavor as buttermilk.

Mary Moon

Marietta, Georgia

MARY MOON DAY

When Johnnie Gabriel asked Marietta's retiring cake lady, Mary Moon, if she could buy her recipes to start her own business, Mary responded, "Honey, you can HAVE these recipes! Nobody in my family wants to work this hard anymore!" Mary Moon did work hard. For more than 30 years, the town's preeminent cake lady made dozens of cakes every week to sell to Marietta residents, in addition to working her full-time job as a telephone operator at the Southern Bell Telephone Company, raising her family, and managing her household.

" I was never lonely baking cakes, because people were always coming by and visiting when they'd come to get their orders."

"I would work at Southern Bell from three in the afternoon until about midnight, and then I'd start baking cakes. And then in the day I'd take a little nap if I had to. I loved baking those cakes." Many of her former customers remember how immaculate Mary's house was, with fresh, boxed cakes lining all the tables and counters.

Mary was born in Marietta in 1924, and her father worked at the Coats and Clark Thread Company. She didn't learn to bake as a girl, because, she says, "I didn't have enough time back then!" But while working at Southern Bell, a co-worker, Opal Williams, invited her over to learn how to bake a red velvet cake. "I'd have never baked a single cake if it weren't for her. After that first red velvet cake, Opal said, 'You did real good.' And once she knew she could trust me to do it, she said, 'Now you can bake 'em at home!'"

Mary began baking at home, and word soon spread about her wonderful cakes. "People got to coming by and seeing them, and tasting them, and people started saying, make one for me!" And so she did. Her most popular cakes were lemon-glazed pound cake, hummingbird cake, carrot cake, Italian cream cake, red velvet, and, of course, fresh coconut cake with seven-minute icing. Her husband and her son would crack the coconuts and shell the pecans for her cakes. Mary's home business thrived from the 1940s through the 1980s, when Johnnie Gabriel began baking Mary's recipes. Being the cake lady, Mary said, kept her in touch with her community. "I was never lonely baking cakes, because people were always coming by and visiting when they'd come to get their orders."

Over the course of her life as a cake lady, Mary Moon became so beloved in Marietta that, in 1988, Mayor Vicki Chastain proclaimed "Mary Moon Day." The proclamation read:

> **WHEREAS**, Mary Moon has been diligent in providing City Hall employees with bountiful cakes, thereby allowing them to keep their busy professional and social lives afloat,
>
> **WHEREAS**, Mrs. Moon not only bakes the freshest, most delicious, most sought-after cakes in town but also delivers them to offices throughout City Hall as requested,
>
> **WHEREAS**, she always arrives with a smile and good cheer,
>
> **WHEREAS**, not only her cakes, but her contagious enthusiasm for life has made all our lives (and figures!) richer and fuller,
>
> **AND WHEREAS**, Mrs. Moon exemplifies the "Marietta Good Citizen,"
>
> **NOW THEREFORE**, I, Vicki Chastain, Mayor of the City of Marietta, Georgia, do hereby proclaim Friday, May 27, 1988, as Mary Moon Day in Marietta, in recognition of her service to the City of Marietta and its employees.

Despite being such a celebrated cake lady, Mary remains humble. When Johnnie told Mary how often her customers inquire about Mary's well-being, she responded, "Now isn't that funny that anybody would remember anything like me? That sure does make me feel good and important."

Mary Moon (left) and Johnnie Gabriel (right)

Fresh Coconut Cake

Fresh Coconut Cake is perhaps the most beloved of all Southern cakes, and it's also the one that requires the most effort. Almost every Southerner I know over the age of 40 remembers cracking, peeling, and grating fresh coconuts for his or her mother's cakes. Cracking and grating fresh coconut is labor-intensive and time-consuming, but the rich, fresh, pure-white, raw coconut is worth every minute of hard work. Homemade Seven-Minute Icing adds a beautiful finish—it's unparalleled in its light, fluffy sweetness.

PREP TIME: 15 minutes plus 20 minutes for the coconut (cooling and grating)

BAKING TIME: 20 to 25 minutes, plus 15 minutes for the coconut

DECORATING TIME: 15 minutes

YOU WILL NEED
FOR THE CAKE:

2 sticks (1 cup) butter, softened

2 cups sugar

4 eggs, at room temperature

2 cups all-purpose flour

1 tablespoon baking powder

½ teaspoon salt

1 cup milk, at room temperature

1 teaspoon pure vanilla extract

FOR THE SEVEN-MINUTE ICING:

2 egg whites

1½ cups sugar

2 teaspoons cream of tartar

⅓ cup cold water

Dash of salt

1 teaspoon pure vanilla extract

Fresh, grated meat of 1 coconut

Preheat the oven to 350°F.

PREPARE THE PANS

Spray the bottom and sides of three 9-inch round cake pans liberally with cooking spray. Place the pans on a sheet of parchment paper and trace three circles the same size as the bottoms of the pans. Cut the circles out and place in the bottoms of the greased pans.

MAKE THE BATTER

In the bowl of a stand mixer fitted with the paddle attachment, beat the butter and sugar together until light and fluffy. Add the eggs one at a time, beating the mixture well after each addition. Scrape down the bottom and sides of the bowl, and beat again until the mixture is smooth, light, and creamy.

In a separate bowl, sift together the flour, baking powder, and salt.

Add the flour mixture to the creamed mixture in three batches, alternating with the milk, beginning and ending with the dry ingredients. Add the vanilla. Beat the batter until smooth after each addition.

BAKE THE CAKE

Gently scrape the batter into the pans, distributing all of the batter evenly among the three pans. Place in the preheated oven, and bake for 20 to 25 minutes, or until a knife inserted into the center of the cake comes out clean and the sides of the cake have pulled away from the sides of the pan. Allow the cakes to cool in the pans, then remove from the pans and set aside until you are ready to ice them.

MAKE THE SEVEN-MINUTE ICING

Fill the bottom of a double boiler with water and bring it to a boil. Turn the heat down to medium to maintain a steady simmer. In the top of the double boiler, combine all of the ingredients except the vanilla and the fresh coconut, and beat with an electric handheld mixer (you can also whip the mixture by hand with a whisk) for 7 minutes or until the icing holds a stiff peak. Remove from the heat, add the vanilla, and then beat the icing to incorporate the vanilla.

ASSEMBLE THE CAKE

Trim any uneven areas from the top of the cake layers with a serrated knife to create a level surface on each. Invert the first layer onto a cake plate, parchment side up. Carefully peel the parchment off the cake and throw it away. Spread about 1 cup of the icing generously on the top surface of the cake with an offset spatula, allowing some of the icing to go over the edge and down the sides. Sprinkle ¾ cup of the fresh coconut on top of the icing. Place the second cake layer on top of the first, and repeat the process—removing the parchment paper, spreading the icing, and sprinkling with coconut. Repeat with the third layer, and then cover the sides and top of the cake with all the remaining icing. Using the offset spatula, lightly tap the cake all over to pull up peaks of icing. Cover with the remaining coconut, pressing the coconut onto the sides of the cake with your hands.

Fresh Coconut Cake should be eaten immediately, as the seven-minute icing will break down within a day, and does not freeze.

How to Crack a Coconut

- Preheat the oven to 400°F.

- Use an ice pick to poke a hole in one of the three eyes at the end of the coconut (two of the eyes will be too hard; one will be just soft enough to puncture through). Wiggle the pick around to widen the hole.

- Drain the coconut water through the hole into a bowl. The water should be fresh and taste pleasant (if it is at all greasy or foul-tasting, your coconut is rancid—start over with a fresh coconut).

- Place the coconut on a cookie sheet in the oven. Bake at 400°F for no more than 15 minutes to loosen the hull.

- Remove the coconut from the oven and allow it to cool.

- Beat the coconut with a mallet until the hard outer hull cracks.

- Peel off the hull with your hands, revealing the softer, inner rind.

- Peel the inner rind with a vegetable peeler.

- What remains is the fresh, white coconut meat. Rinse off any debris from the hull, and grate the meat with a cheese grater.

Olga Perez

Asheville, North Carolina

UNA MUJER AFORTUNADA
(A LUCKY WOMAN)

Unlike many Southern cake ladies, Olga Perez didn't learn to bake as a child. Growing up in the rural Mexican state of Hidalgo, she says that her mother "would never, never, never let me in the kitchen! I would say, 'Mom, can I help you?' because she was a very busy woman. But she would say, 'No, go study. This is not for you.'" Olga instead learned to bake in high school, where, given the choice between science class and baking class, she chose baking. Olga loved learning and wanted to go to college, but when she became pregnant, she found that she did not have the support she needed to continue her studies. Instead, she had to drop out of high school. She married her daughter's father and followed him to the United States. Eventually, the rest of her family also ended up in North Carolina.

As a young mother in a foreign culture, Olga began to experiment with baking. "I started trying to remember everything that I used to do in school. I started making cakes for my family, and they liked what I did. I love the feeling of baking. I feel a lot of creativity. I started to add things—a little of this, a little of that—people liked that. My brothers and sisters said, 'Why don't you sell your cakes and your flan?' 'I don't sell them,' I would say. But they were always asking me for more and more. I didn't have the money for the ingredients, so I told them that if they wanted me to make them a cake, they would have to bring me the ingredients. But eventually they started to pay for the cakes. They wanted them for birthday parties, so I had to learn how to make larger quantities. That's when I decided that I had to buy all the materials that I needed, and I started making and selling them more. It is special for me, when all the guests at a party are saying, 'Oh, I love the cake. It's the best cake that I've ever tasted!'"

Olga Perez's pastel de tres leches (three milks cake), flan, and Mexican gelatins are in high demand now in the Emma community of West Asheville, and have provided her a means to help support her family. Olga says, "The difference between my tres leches cake and the ones that you will find in the Mexican stores is that the store-bought cakes they prepare a couple of days ahead of time, and they are too soaking wet. And they use jams or jellies, artificial things, and they use a lot of dyes, and food coloring. But with my cakes, you know, maybe I don't know how to decorate them perfectly and beautifully, but I think mine are better."

" I love the feeling of baking. I feel a lot of creativity."

Growing a home baking business, along with raising her three daughters, keeps Olga busy and happy, but she has not forgotten her dream of furthering her education. "I would like to go back to school and learn more, but really, I don't have the time. So selling cakes is something that I can do right now and bring in money. But I have a hope that one day my husband will be able to get me my papers and I will go to school and get a better job. Like all Mexican women, I'm trying to get ahead." She adds, "I know Hispanic women who are tied to their husbands, and if their husband says no, they don't move; they are stuck. I am not one of those women. I told my husband, 'I can do this. I want to grow. If you want to grow with me, you are welcome to do that. If not, adios.'

"My family is the thing that I am most proud of in my life. My husband is marvelous and we are a very united family. We don't have a lot, but we have a lot of love. So maybe we don't need as much money, because we have our health, we have a home, I have my beautiful daughters, and I have my parents and my brothers and sisters close. Maybe those are things that other people don't have. I am rich in that regard. I feel like a lucky woman."

Special thanks to Ada Volkmer for translation assistance.

Pastel de Tres Leches

Pastel de Tres Leches (Three Milks Cake) is popular throughout Latin America. The cake is somewhat dense so that it's able to maintain its texture while soaked with the three milks. All that milk and a whipped cream topping make for a sweet and delightfully messy cake. The fruits used in Pastel de Tres Leches vary by region and season, but Olga makes hers with blueberries and strawberries. Plan to bake the cake the day before serving it, so you can soak the layers overnight.

PREP TIME: 15 minutes

BAKING TIME: 25 to 30 minutes

COOLING/NONACTIVE PREP TIME: 8 hours to overnight

DECORATING TIME: 15 minutes

YOU WILL NEED
FOR THE CAKE:

1 stick (½ cup) salted butter, softened

1 cup sugar

5 large eggs, at room temperature

1 teaspoon pure vanilla extract

1½ cups all-purpose flour

1½ teaspoons baking powder

1 (14-ounce) can sweetened condensed milk

1 (12-ounce) can evaporated milk

1 cup whole milk

FOR THE WHIPPED CREAM TOPPING:

1 pint heavy whipping cream

¼ cup sugar

1 teaspoon pure vanilla extract

1 pint fresh strawberries

1 pint fresh blueberries

Preheat the oven to 350°F.

PREPARE THE PAN

Spray a 10-inch square cake pan liberally with cooking spray. Lay a sheet of parchment paper in the bottom of the pan and up the sides.

MIX THE BATTER

Combine the butter and the sugar in the bowl of a stand mixer, and beat on low speed until creamed. Stop the mixer and, using the rubber spatula, scrape down the paddle, sides, and bottom of the bowl. Add the eggs, one at a time, beating at a low speed after each addition. Add the vanilla. Beat on low speed for 3 to 5 minutes, or until the mixture is light and fluffy. Stop the mixer twice during mixing to scrape down the paddle and the bottom and sides of the bowl.

Measure the flour and the baking powder, and place them in the sifter, over a separate, clean bowl. Sift the flour and baking powder together. Add the flour mixture to the creamed mixture in three parts, scraping between each addition, and then beating until fully combined.

BAKE THE CAKE

Gently scrape the batter into the lined pan, spreading it into the corners of the pan. Place the pan in the preheated oven and bake for 25 to 30 minutes, or until the surface of the cake springs back when touched with your finger, a knife inserted into the center of the cake comes out clean, and the sides of the cake have pulled away from the sides of the pan.

SOAK THE CAKE

When the cake is completely cool, gently perforate the entire surface with a fork. Combine the sweetened condensed milk, the evaporated milk, and the whole milk in a bowl and stir. While the cake is still in the pan, pour the mixture slowly over the top of the cake, and allow it to evenly saturate the entire cake. Place the soaking cake layer in the refrigerator for 8 hours or overnight.

MAKE THE WHIPPED CREAM TOPPING

In the bowl of a stand mixer with a whisk attachment, whip the heavy cream, sugar, and vanilla at the highest speed, until the mixture becomes light and fluffy and can hold a stiff peak. (Be careful not to overbeat the mixture, or it will become butter.)

Slice the strawberries. Transfer 2 cups of the whipped cream to a separate bowl. Add 1 cup of the strawberries and 1 cup of the blueberries to the separate cream, and mix with a rubber spatula until the fruit is evenly distributed in the cream.

PREPARE THE CAKE LAYERS FOR ICING

Line a large plate or tray with waxed paper. Invert the cake onto the waxed paper, allowing the milk that spills out to pool at the bottom of the cake. Use a serrated knife to slice the cake in half horizontally so you have two even layers of cake. Place the first layer on a serving plate. Handling the wet soaked layers can be tricky; if they tear while transporting them to the serving platter, simply piece them back together.

With a spatula, scrape the fruit and whipped cream mixture on top of the first layer, spreading the whipped cream evenly on the surface. Place the second cake layer on top of the first, and pour any of the milk mixture that has run out into the waxed paper back onto the cake. With the remaining whipped cream, cover the top and sides of the cake. Use the remaining fruit to garnish the cake.

Tres Leches Cake should be kept cold and served immediately.

Olga's Kitchen Wisdom

There are many variations on Pastel de Tres Leches. Try substituting blackberries, peaches, or mangos for the strawberries and blueberries. Many bakers include a few tablespoons of rum with the milk mixture. Feel free to experiment with this fresh, creamy, summertime dessert.

The New South

In recent years, many parts of the South have seen a dramatic increase in the number of immigrants arriving from Mexico and other parts of Latin America. Like the other ethnic groups that have settled here over the centuries, Latino immigrants are influencing the South socially and economically, and, like other immigrant groups before them, Latino immigrants face both social and economic challenges and barriers. The preservation of traditional foods is one way that immigrants are surviving and thriving in a foreign culture—and a way that the culinary landscape of the South is enriched. For Olga Perez, baking and selling traditional Mexican Tres Leches Cake from her home has become a means for her to support her family economically and to preserve and pass down a connection to her home in Mexico.

Lisa Goldstein

Celo, North Carolina

TOO MUCH OF A GOOD THING IS WONDERFUL

Lisa Goldstein has been baking and decorating cakes for community celebrations for the same 53 years she's been attending births as a midwife. As a teenager, she lived in Washington, DC, with her grandmother, who taught her to make cakes from scratch. "She really liked to make the good stuff—she would bake a cake from a box and put it side by side with a made-from-scratch cake and say, 'Now, taste the difference.' We made Italian cream cakes, fresh coconut cakes, chocolate cakes—you name it. It was about that time that I started to bake and decorate cakes for all my friends' birthdays, as presents." Lisa says her philosophy is "A cake is a symbol of love. It's a symbol of giving; it says, 'I made this for you, because I love you so much.'"

It was as a preteen that Lisa began her training as a midwife: She was just 12 when she attended her first birth while living in Italy (where her father was stationed with the Navy). Lisa was called to help an Italian midwife with a home birth in the apartment building where her family lived. The experience changed her life. Though she moved every couple of years growing up, in 1973, when Lisa, her husband, and children moved to the rural mountains of Western North Carolina from Philadelphia, she knew she had found her home. She and her husband, Gavriel, built a home in the Celo community and worked as house parents at the Arthur Morgan School, where Lisa taught French cooking and sex education as she built her midwifery practice.

> " A cake is a symbol of love. It's a symbol of giving; it says, 'I made this for you, because I love you so much.'"

It took a little time to be embraced by the local community, but she says, "One of the neat things about mountain people all over the world is that they want to do things their own way. If you raise the price of flour, they'll grow corn and make cornbread. They don't want to be put down, but if you have a skill that they respect, like helping their sister have a baby, the whole family will then think, 'well, she looks funny but she's OK.'" Starting out, Lisa practiced midwifery the old way: with lots of experience but no legal certification. By 1983, a local grassroots campaign convinced the state legislature to "grandmother in" Lisa as a legal midwife—she became the only legal non-nurse midwife in North Carolina and has since gone on to become a certified nurse midwife.

Over the decades she has spent attending births in the mountains of rural Yancy, Avery, Madison, and Mitchell counties, she has also made cakes: fantastical, outrageously decorated wedding cakes and birthday cakes for friends and loved ones. Chocolate cherubs, hard candies, heart-shaped lollipops, beads, icing roses, fresh flowers, candles, sparkly paper, and fountains are just a few of the elements Lisa incorporates into her multi-tiered confections. When asked

about the inspiration behind her over-the-top, elaborate cake decorations, Lisa simply responds, "Too much of a good thing is wonderful, you know." Lisa's youngest son, Jesse Goldstein, would often stay up with her all night to work on the wedding cakes. Jesse recalls the rich smell of almond extract from his mother's kitchen, and her fearlessness when it came to a challenge—whether in cake, or other realms of life—"She would just tackle anything. It was a great lesson for me: If you're gonna be a bear, be a grizzly." Jesse is now a chef, and a manager at the well-known Loveless Café in Nashville, Tennessee.

" Too much of a good thing is wonderful, you know."

While Lisa's elaborate celebration cakes are beautiful, perhaps her most meaningful, sweet, and poignant cakes are the ones she bakes for women while attending their births at home. "I always bake a birthday cake for the baby when I'm attending a home birth. It's part of my job—a big pot of soup for the family when everything is over, and a birthday cake."

Lisa's life has always been about love and nurturing—from helping women have babies, to sharing her knowledge of plant medicine, to cooking and baking. Baking for other people has always been a part of that. She says, "Life can be going to hell, but if you have a beautiful cake presented to you, for a moment, everything is perfect." Each year, Lisa's birthday is celebrated with a "Chocolate Party," an elaborate spread of all things chocolate, baked by her friends and family, so the many people who love Lisa have a chance to return the favor—and bake beautiful cakes full of love for her.

In 2005, I was lucky enough to have Lisa attend the birth of my son. Like thousands of mothers (and grandmothers, as Lisa has now attended multiple generations of births in some families) in these mountains where I live, I've grown to love Lisa as a friend, a caregiver, and a mentor. Though she didn't bake me a cake (we were in the hospital in Spruce Pine), she did knit my son a hat while I was in labor.

Carrot Cake

Carrot cake is a favorite of young and old alike, and it's perfect for a birthday celebration. Lisa always replaces some of the white flour in her recipes with whole wheat flour, so that, as she says, "We can pretend that it's health food."

PREP TIME: 20 minutes
BAKING TIME: 30 to 35 minutes
COOLING TIME: about 1 hour
DECORATING TIME: 15 to 20 minutes

YOU WILL NEED
FOR THE CAKE:

2 sticks (1 cup) salted butter, at room temperature

1¾ cups sugar

¼ cup molasses

4 large eggs, at room temperature

1½ cups all-purpose flour

1½ cups whole wheat flour

½ teaspoon baking soda

1 tablespoon baking powder

2 teaspoons cinnamon

1 teaspoon allspice

1 teaspoon nutmeg

1½ cups buttermilk, at room temperature

2 cups grated carrots

Zest of 1 lemon

FOR THE ICING:

2 packages (1 pound) cream cheese, softened

1 stick (½ cup) salted butter, softened

1 teaspoon pure vanilla extract

5 cups powdered sugar

Preheat the oven to 350°F.

PREPARE THE PANS

Spray the bottom and sides of three 9-inch round cake pans liberally with cooking spray. Place the pans on a sheet of parchment paper and trace three circles the same size as the bottoms of the pans. Cut the circles out and place in the bottoms of the greased pans.

MAKE THE BATTER

Cream the butter, sugar, and molasses together in the bowl of a stand mixer fitted with the paddle attachment until light and fluffy. While beating the mixture on low speed, add the eggs, one at a time, beating after each addition. Using a rubber spatula, scrape down the bottom and sides of the bowl, and beat again until the mixture is smooth, light, and creamy.

Sift the flours, baking soda, baking powder, and spices together into a separate bowl.

With the blender on low speed, alternately add the dry ingredients and the buttermilk to the creamed mixture in three parts, beginning and ending with the dry ingredients. Scrape down the bottom and sides of the bowl several times. Mix lightly but thoroughly between each addition, until ingredients are just combined.

Add the carrots and lemon zest, and stir by hand until combined.

BAKE THE CAKE

Gently scrape the batter into the pans, dividing the batter evenly between the three pans. Place in the preheated oven, and bake for 30 to 35 minutes, or until a knife inserted into the center of the cake comes out clean and the sides of the cake have pulled away from the sides of the pan. Allow the cakes to cool for 20 minutes before removing the layers from the pans and setting on a wire rack to finish cooling.

MAKE THE ICING

Cream the cream cheese and butter together in the bowl of the stand mixer, on low speed. Beat until the mixture is smooth and creamy and no lumps of butter remain. Add and combine the vanilla. Add the powdered sugar 1 cup at a time, blending on low speed until fully incorporated. Using the rubber spatula, scrape down the paddle, sides, and bottom of the bowl. Beat the mixture on medium speed until light and fluffy.

ASSEMBLE THE CAKE

When the cake layers are completely cool, trim off any uneven areas from the tops of the cake layers with a serrated knife.

Invert the first layer onto a cake plate, so that the parchment side is up. Carefully peel the parchment off of the cake and throw it away. Spread about 1 cup of the cream cheese icing on the top surface of the cake with an offset spatula, pushing the icing over the edges of the layer and creating an even coat of icing. Place the second cake layer on top of the first and repeat the process—removing the parchment paper and spreading the icing. Repeat with the third layer, and then cover the sides with the icing.

Carrot Cake can be kept covered at room temperature for up to three days, and can be kept refrigerated for up to a week.

Natural Food Coloring

Make your celebration cake shine by adding natural food-based dyes to your decorative icings. In these photos, Spirulina powder was used for green, turmeric for yellow, beet powder for pink, and turmeric and beet powder for orange. As with liquid food coloring, add these food-based powders to the icing a little bit at a time to figure out the quantities you prefer for deepness or lightness of hue.

Poppy Seed Cake with Almond Buttercream Icing

This is Lisa's favorite cake to bake for weddings. Rich with almond flavor, poppy seeds, and cardamom, it makes a special, and somewhat exotic, treat.

PREP TIME: 25 to 30 minutes
BAKING TIME: about 35 minutes
COOLING TIME: about 1½ hours
DECORATING TIME: 15 to 20 minutes

YOU WILL NEED
FOR THE CAKE:

- 6 large eggs, separated, at room temperature
- ½ teaspoon cream of tartar
- 2 sticks (1 cup) salted butter, softened
- 2 cups sugar
- ½ cup honey
- 2 cups milk, at room temperature
- 2 tablespoons vinegar
- 1 tablespoon pure almond extract
- 1½ cups all-purpose flour
- 1½ cups whole wheat flour
- 1 tablespoon baking powder
- ¼ cup cornstarch
- 1 teaspoon nutmeg
- 1 teaspoon cinnamon
- A pinch of cardamom
- ½ cup poppy seeds

FOR THE ICING:

- 2 sticks (1 cup) butter, softened
- 5 cups confectioner's sugar
- 1 teaspoon pure vanilla extract
- 1 teaspoon pure almond extract
- 4 tablespoons half-and-half, plus more if needed

Preheat the oven to 350°F.

PREPARE THE PANS

Spray the bottom and sides of three 9-inch round cake pans liberally with cooking spray. Place the pans on a sheet of parchment paper and trace three circles the same size as the bottoms of the pans. Cut the circles out and place in the bottoms of the greased pans.

MAKE THE BATTER

In the bowl of a stand mixer fitted with the whisk, whip the egg whites together with the cream of tartar on high speed, until soft peaks form. Set aside.

In a separate bowl of a stand mixer, cream the butter, sugar, and honey together until light and fluffy. While beating the mixture on low speed, add the egg yolks one at a time, beating after each addition. Scrape down the bottom and sides of the bowl, and beat again until the mixture is smooth, light, and creamy.

In a bowl, combine the milk, vinegar, and almond extract, and set aside.

Sift the flours, baking powder, cornstarch, nutmeg, cinnamon, and cardamom together into a separate bowl.

Add the dry mixture to the creamed mixture in three parts, alternating with the liquid mixture, and mixing lightly but thoroughly between each addition, until ingredients are just combined.

Add the poppy seeds, folding them in by hand until combined. Quickly re-whisk the egg whites by hand if they have separated, then fold them into the batter in three batches.

BAKE THE CAKE

Gently scrape the batter into the pans, distributing all of the batter evenly between the three pans. Place in the preheated oven, and bake for 30 to 45 minutes, or until a knife inserted into the center of the cake comes out clean and the sides of the cake have pulled away from the sides of the pan. Allow the cakes to cool in the pans, then remove from the pans and set aside until you are ready to ice them.

MAKE THE ICING

Cream the butter and the confectioner's sugar together in the bowl of a stand mixer fitted with the paddle until it makes a thick paste. Add and combine the vanilla and almond extract. Add the half-and-half, 1 tablespoon at a time, blending on low speed until fully incorporated. Add more if needed for a creamy, fluffy consistency. Using the rubber spatula, scrape down the paddle, sides, and bottom of the bowl. Beat the mixture again until no lumps remain.

ASSEMBLE THE CAKE

When the cake layers are completely cool, trim off any uneven areas from the tops with a serrated knife. Invert the first layer onto a cake plate, parchment side up. Carefully peel the parchment off of the cake and throw it away. Spread about ½ cup of the buttercream icing on the top surface of the cake with an offset spatula, pushing the icing over the edges of the layer and creating an even coat of icing. Place the second cake layer on top of the first and repeat the process—removing the parchment paper and spreading the icing. Repeat with the third layer, and then cover the sides with the icing.

Poppy Seed Cake can be kept covered at room temperature for up to three days, and can be kept refrigerated for up to a week.

Dye Scott-Rhodan

Hilton Head Island, South Carolina

GULLAH IS YA 'UM (GULLAH IS HERE)

When I first met Dye Scott-Rhodan, owner of Dye's Gullah Fixin's on Hilton Head Island, South Carolina, I asked whether she made her cakes from scratch. She responded, "How else would I make 'em? I only know butter, sugar, flour, and eggs. That's all I know. We make bread pudding, blackberry dump, pound cakes, sweet potato pound cake, old fashioned caramel, pecan coconut pound cake, bundt cakes, fig cakes—and everything, icings and everything, is from scratch. We always do everything from scratch, because we had to. We catch crabs, we shell our own butter beans—there's a lot of labor that goes into it. Nowadays, they calling it organic. But we been doing organic all our lives. I just wish they'd have paid my daddy two dollars for a cucumber."

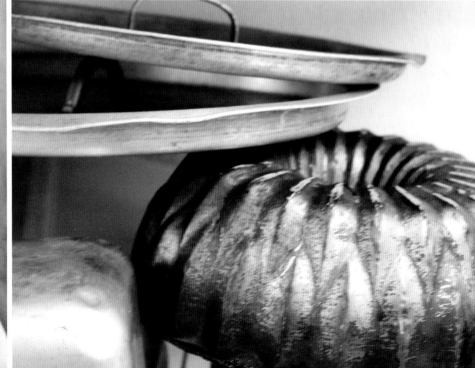

Dye's passion for food is obvious, but her passion for her native culture, the Gullah people of the Low Country of South Carolina and Georgia, is even greater. "I'm an old-fashioned country cook. I don't know if you've ever touched this culture, but this culture's called Gullah. We're West Africans brought into slavery. We were brought here to cook, raise children, and farm, so we really invented [Southern] cooking before anybody else." Dye was born and raised in the Gullah community of rural Ridgeland, South Carolina, about 30 miles inland from Hilton Head Island. Her father was a farmer, and her mother was a cook. Her family raised most of what they ate, going to the store for one primary Gullah food staple: rice. Dye worked as a cook in the school cafeteria before starting a catering business on the side that eventually grew to be Dye's Gullah Fixin's. Her busy restaurant serves lunch and dinner to visitors to the island. Her business is a way for her not only to make a living but also to preserve her community's traditions and educate the world about the Gullah people.

"My grandmother made old-fashioned cakes, pies, and dumps in the cast iron skillet. We always had cakes. We always made desserts, because we had lots of fig trees, peach trees, plenty of blackberries and blueberries—we'd go into the woods in the morning and come back with baskets full by lunchtime. Special occasions we would do butter cakes and bundt cakes." Dye believes that you have to have your heart in the right place to bake a good cake: "I always feel that when anybody cook a recipe or bake a cake or whatever they do, it's the love within them that's formed into that recipe. That's what make it taste the way it do. I could give you a recipe, but if you don't have that kind of love, it's not going to taste like mine. The biggest thing is to have holiness in you, because God made all of us one. You've got to treat others the way you want to be treated, because you can't do wrong and expect to be right."

" I always feel that when anybody cook a recipe or bake a cake or whatever they do, it's the love within them that's formed into that recipe."

Dye's goal is to have her own Gullah-themed cooking show on the Food Network to reclaim the credit for country cooking she feels the Gullah community is owed. She publishes a magazine, called *Gullah Is Ya 'Um (Gullah Is Here)*, celebrating Gullah culture, history, and folklore, and highlighting events and businesses within the Gullah community, and she is writing her own cookbook. She's also developing a line of Gullah seasonings, named in honor of her father, called Daddy Tuke's Nappy Pickin's and Thangs to sell online and in her restaurant. She hosts gospel singing and Gullah storytelling events at the restaurant, and she's bringing up the next generation, including her six-year-old twin nieces Malaysia and Ashiana, to cook, bake, and be self-reliant, in the tradition of the Gullah people.

Low Country Geechee

Gullah culture is unique to the African-American descendants of West African slaves that were brought to the Low Country and sea islands of South Carolina and Georgia to farm rice. Gullah people living on sea islands farmed, fished, crafted, cooked, and told stories in the old ways, resisted assimilation, and maintained many aspects of African tradition, spirituality, and language. The Gullah language (also called Low Country Geechee), is still spoken by over 250,000 people. Once ridiculed as broken English, it's now recognized for its unique blending of African and English languages, grammar, and sentence structure. The beauty and resilience of the language is a source of fierce pride for the people who make up the Gullah community. Dye gives examples of common phrases spoken in the Gullah language: "Icin' de cake an' de chillum biddin' fo' de spone." (When I'm icing the cake, the children beg for the spoon.) And "I'se bakin' ebery day dey's best de ol' fashion way." (I'm baking every day; it's best the old-fashioned way.)

Gullah Dirty Cake

Dye Scott-Rhodan recalls that Gullah Dirty Cake was everyone's favorite when she was a child. "I remember everybody fighting over the last piece, and fighting over who would lick the spoons. The recipe was passed down to me through my aunt, from my great-grandmother. That dark chocolate reminds us of the black dirt, so we call it dirty cake."

PREP TIME: 20 minutes
BAKING TIME: 35 minutes
COOLING TIME: 1 hour
DECORATING TIME: 20 minutes

YOU WILL NEED
FOR THE CAKE:

- ½ cup lard (see page 130 for more on lard)
- 1¼ cups sugar
- 1 cup packed brown sugar
- 4 large eggs, at room temperature
- 3 ounces unsweetened baker's chocolate, melted
- 2½ cups cake flour
- 1 teaspoon baking soda
- ½ teaspoon salt
- 1¼ cups buttermilk
- 1 teaspoon pure vanilla extract

FOR THE ICING:

- 3 sticks (1½ cups) salted butter
- 1½ cups cocoa powder
- 1¼ cups milk
- 3 teaspoons pure vanilla extract
- 15 cups powdered sugar

Preheat the oven to 325°F.

PREPARE THE PANS

Spray three 8-inch round cake pans liberally with cooking spray. Place the pans on a sheet of parchment paper, and trace three circles the same size as the bottoms of the pans. Cut the circles out and place in the bottoms of the greased pans.

MAKE THE BATTER

In the bowl of a stand mixer fitted with the paddle attachement, beat the lard slowly. Add the sugars, beating at medium speed until creamed, light, and fluffy. Stop the mixer and, using a rubber spatula, scrape down the paddle, sides, and bottom of the bowl. Add the eggs to the mixture, one at a time, stopping the mixer to scrape down the bowl after each addition. Add the chocolate. Make sure that it has cooled slightly, but is still melted.

Measure the flour, baking soda, and salt, and place them in the sifter, over a separate, clean bowl. Sift the ingredients together.

Add a third of the flour mixture to the creamed mixture and beat slowly until just combined. Add half of the buttermilk, and beat slowly until just combined. Repeat, alternating between the flour mixture and the buttermilk, ending with flour mixture. Add the vanilla and combine. Stop the mixer and thoroughly scrape down the paddle, sides, and bottom of the bowl, and continue to beat the mixture on low speed until all the ingredients are fully incorporated and the cake batter is light and uniform in color and texture. Be careful not to beat the mixture any more after the ingredients are all smoothly incorporated, however, as this will toughen the batter and create air tunnels in the finished cake.

BAKE THE CAKE

Divide the batter evenly among the three pans. Place in the preheated oven, and bake for 35 minutes, or until a knife inserted in the center of the cake comes out clean and the sides of the cake have pulled away from the sides of the pan. Set the pans aside and allow the cakes to cool completely.

MAKE THE ICING

Mix the butter, cocoa, and milk in a saucepan and heat on medium low heat, stirring, until the butter melts and the ingredients are fully combined. Remove from the heat, and add the vanilla. Place the chocolate mixture into the bowl of the stand mixer with the paddle, and whip until completely cooled; if you add the sugar to the chocolate mixture while warm, it will melt and become sticky and not fluffy. Add the powdered sugar, a cup at a time, scraping down the bowl periodically, until fluffy and spreadable.

ASSEMBLE THE CAKE

Invert the first layer onto a cake plate, so that the parchment side is up. Carefully peel the parchment off of the cake and throw it away. Spread about 1½ cups of the icing on the top surface of the cake with an offset spatula, pushing the icing over the edges of the layer and creating an even coat of icing. Place the second cake layer on top of the first and repeat the process— removing the parchment paper and spreading the icing. Repeat with the third layer, and then cover the sides with the icing.

Dye's Kitchen Wisdom

If the icing is too liquid and hard to work with, simply let it stand, whipping occasionally, until it begins to thicken. Also, if the icing is too soft, the layers can shift while decorating; pop the filled cake into the refrigerator to firm up so the layers don't slide while you're icing the exterior.

Gullah Dirty Cake can be kept covered at room temperature up to three days or up to a week if refrigerated.

Jessica Grossman

Charleston, South Carolina

RED SHOES AND BLACK MAGIC

When Jessica Grossman's friend Dana Berlin told her that she had but one cake (a pound cake) to serve on the opening night of her new Charleston restaurant, Jessica decided that that just wouldn't do. "I'll bring you a chocolate cake," Jessica remembers saying. "I brought a Black Magic Cake. She came to me at the end of the night and said, 'Hey! I need two more for tomorrow, and four for the weekend. And what else can you make?' So I said, 'I can make Pecan Pie!'" She did, and that's how she "accidentally" became the baker for the now very popular Jestine's Kitchen and began what she calls her mission to find the "kookiest, most oddball Southern recipes I could get my hands on." Jessica and her signature red shoes (shiny patent leather Mary Janes) have been running the show two doors down at Jestine's Sweet Shop ever since.

butterscotch

black magic

When Jessica says kooky, she means it. She loves collecting mid-century cookbooks and recipes for such gems as Coca-Cola Cake, Tomato Soup Cake, and Fruit Cocktail Cake. One of her favorites is Jud's Impress Your Friends Kahlúa Cake, which includes cake mix, coffee, and Kahlúa, among other things. Her friends are now in the habit of sending her quirky Southern recipes like Mountain Dew Apple Cobbler (sliced apples, canned crescent rolls, sugar, butter, and Mountain Dew). A fondness for oddball Southernisms was natural for Jessica. Growing up as a Jewish girl in Florence, South Carolina, the daughter of a Hungarian immigrant father (who was also a Holocaust survivor) and a Swedish immigrant mother, Jessica often felt like an outsider. And, being that Southerners and Southern cooks often define themselves by the ways in which they are different from the rest of the world, Jessica says that her interest in "weird" food was a natural fit. "We were always weird. Growing up, you think that everybody's mom makes the same dishes, and then you realize that they don't. There were always 'variety meats' around the house, like Swedish beefsteak, tongue, and liver pâte. And my father used to make goulash."

"Sweets make people happy. And, as far as I'm concerned, one of the greatest things I can do, and what I'm good at, is making people happy."

Though she felt different growing up, Jessica describes Florence as "one of those Southern towns that didn't know how small it was." She learned to embrace her outsider status and quirky Southern baking, too. Though she took up baking on her own at an early age, primarily through her Easy-Bake Oven, it took culinary school for Jessica to discover that she knew what she was doing all along. She says, "When Dana was trying to convince me to open the Sweet Shop, I thought,

'That's crazy! I don't know how to do that! What do I know about baking, me and my Easy-Bake Oven?' But we just went for it. Eventually, I decided I should go to school to fill in the gaps of my knowledge, and, turns out, I knew a lot already. Culinary school was an expensive lesson in confidence, but it was worth it."

Jessica says, "Sweets make people happy. And, as far as I'm concerned, one of the greatest things I can do, and what I'm good at, is making people happy. I always feel bad for people like the meter maid, because no one is happy, ever, to see her coming. But when I come walking in, people can't wait to see what I'm bringing! So it's a pretty great situation to be in, particularly when times are tough." In addition to making the customers at Jestine's Sweet Shop happy, she also won the heart of her true love by sending him Black Magic Cake in the mail: "I plied him with desserts when he was living in Arkansas. We've now been together for 13 years."

Jessica makes people happy in many other ways: She has become a mentor for aspiring Cake Lady Nakesha Rivers, who has been an employee at Jestine's Sweet Shop for a year and a half. Kesha has been learning to bake from Jessica: "I'm just lucky," Kesha says. "I started off as front counter help, and now I'm baking. I liked to cook but never did any baking. I learned everything about baking from Jessica. Now, when she's not here, I'm just here baking. It's fun, it's relaxing."

A letter from a young customer sums up Jessica Grossman's relationship to cakes and making people happy: "Dear Jessica, Thank you so much for that fantastic cake. It was the best thing I've ever tasted in the entire world."

Hummingbird Cake

Rich and sweet, Hummingbird Cake is one of Jessica Grossman's favorite, quintessentially Southern recipes. This moist cake containing pineapple, bananas, and pecans is also known in the South as Never Ending Cake, Nothing Left Cake, and Jamaican Cake.

PREP TIME: 15 minutes
BAKING TIME: 20 to 25 minutes
COOLING TIME: 1½ hours
DECORATING TIME: 15 minutes

YOU WILL NEED
FOR THE CAKE:

- 3 large eggs, at room temperature
- 2 cups sugar
- ¾ cup vegetable oil
- 1½ teaspoons pure vanilla extract
- 3 cups all-purpose flour
- 1 teaspoon baking soda
- ½ teaspoon salt
- 1 teaspoon cinnamon
- 1 (8-ounce) can crushed pineapple, not drained
- 1¾ cups mashed ripe bananas
- 1 cup chopped pecans

FOR THE CREAM CHEESE ICING:

- 1 stick (½ cup) salted butter, softened
- 2 packages (1 pound) cream cheese, softened
- 1 teaspoon pure vanilla extract
- 5 cups powdered sugar

Preheat the oven to 350°F.

PREPARE THE PANS

Spray the bottom and sides of three 9-inch round cake pans liberally with cooking spray. Place the pans on a sheet of parchment paper and trace three circles the same size as the bottoms of the pans. Cut the circles out and place them in the bottoms of the greased pans.

MIX THE BATTER

In the bowl of a stand mixer fitted with the paddle attachment, beat the eggs and sugar together until light and fluffy. While beating the mixture on low speed, add the vegetable oil in a slow, steady stream. Add the vanilla, and beat until incorporated. Scrape down the bottom and sides of the bowl, and beat again until the mixture is smooth, light, and creamy.

Sift the flour, baking soda, salt, and cinnamon together into a separate bowl, and then add these dry ingredients, in three parts, to the creamed mixture, mixing lightly but thoroughly between each addition and scraping down the bowl, until ingredients are just combined.

Add the pineapple (liquid included), banana, and pecans to the batter, and stir by hand with the spatula until all the ingredients are incorporated.

BAKE THE CAKE

Gently scrape the batter to distribute all of it evenly among the three pans. Place in the preheated oven, and bake for 20 to 25 minutes, or until a knife inserted into the center of the cake comes out clean and the sides of the cake have pulled away from the sides of the pan. Allow the cakes to cool in the pans, then remove them from the pans and set them aside until you're ready to ice them.

MAKE THE ICING

Cream the butter and the cream cheese together in the bowl of a stand mixer with the paddle on low speed. Beat until the mixture is smooth and creamy and no lumps of butter remain. Add and combine the vanilla. Add the powdered sugar, 1 cup at a time, blending on low speed until fully incorporated. Using a rubber spatula, scrape down the paddle, sides, and bottom of the bowl. Beat the mixture on medium speed until light and fluffy. If the icing gets too soft to hold a peak, chill it briefly in the refrigerator, stirring often, until it thickens.

ASSEMBLE THE CAKE

When the cake layers are completely cool, trim any uneven areas from the top of the layers with a serrated knife to create a level surface on each. Invert the first layer onto a cake plate, parchment side up. Carefully peel the parchment off the cake and throw it away. Spread about 1½ cups of the cream cheese icing on the top surface of the cake with an offset spatula, pushing the icing over the edges of the layer and creating an even coat of icing. Place the second cake layer on top of the first and repeat the process of removing the parchment paper and spreading the icing. Repeat with the third layer, and then cover the sides with the icing.

Hummingbird Cake can be kept covered at room temperature up to three days or up to a week if refrigerated.

How to Name a Cake

Hummingbird Cake is an example of the way many food names evolve: haphazardly and with no traceable history, leaving lots of room for romantic conjecture. Here are just a few of the many (all equally plausible) explanations for the name Hummingbird Cake.

- Hummingbird Cake originated in Jamaica, where the national bird is the swallow-tail hummingbird, also known as the doctor bird.
- Hummingbird Cake is so named because the hummingbird, with its love of nectar, is a symbol of sweetness.
- Hummingbird Cake is so delicious that it makes people "hum" with delight.

Dried Pineapple Flowers

This can be a slow process, but well worth the pre-planning. Make the flowers a day or two ahead to accommodate varying drying times for the pineapple. Even though these slices are going in the oven, it's good to think of this more as a drying process rather than a baking process.

YOU WILL NEED:

1 large or 2 small pineapples, more firm than ripe

Very sharp knife

Kitchen scissors

Parchment paper

Baking sheet(s)

Wire cooling rack(s)

Heat the oven to 200°F.

Peel the pineapple by shaving off the outer rind with a knife (a serrated knife is best), and then remove the deepest "eyes" from the outer edge.

Place the pineapple on its side and slice it into thin cross-sections, the thinner the better!

With scissors, make ½-inch-deep v-shaped cuts at 1- to 1½-inch intervals around the circular edge of each slice—you can aim these cuts at any remaining "eyes."

Place the slices on parchment-lined baking sheets and bake for 30 to 45 minutes.

TIP: The slices will dry faster if you place them on wire cooling racks laid over parchment-lined sheets.

Flip the slices over, repositioning them away from damp spots on the parchment, and bake for another 30 to 45 minutes.

If the edges begin to brown, reduce the heat to 185°F to dry more slowly.

After 1 to 2 hours of drying time in the oven, check the slices. If they're not almost leather-like, you may need to add more bake-and-turn cycles.

Once they're dehydrated, remove the slices from the oven, place them on wire racks to cool, and continue the drying process for 3 to 12 more hours. This time varies due to the pineapple's water content, the thickness of the slices, and environmental humidity.

To use the pineapple slices on the cake, trim away any dark edges, then mold them into flower shapes by holding each slice's center tightly in the crook of your thumb and index finger and pulling up on the sides to form a cup-like shape. "Plant" each flower in the cake's icing.

Refrigerate leftover pineapple flowers in an airtight container for about a week.

Peanut Butter & Banana Cupcakes

This cupcake's moist, sweet banana cake is nicely balanced by the fluffy peanut butter icing. (Elvis's favorite comfort food was a peanut butter and banana sandwich—the combination is a Southern tradition.) A banana chip makes a very pretty garnish for these cupcakes.

PREP TIME: 20 minutes
BAKING TIME: 15 to 20 minutes
COOLING TIME: about 45 minutes
DECORATING TIME: 15 minutes

YOU WILL NEED
FOR THE CUPCAKES:

- 2 eggs, at room temperature
- ¾ cup packed light brown sugar
- ¾ cup sugar
- ½ cup vegetable oil
- 2 teaspoons pure vanilla extract
- 1 cup mashed ripe bananas
- ¾ cup smooth peanut butter
- 2 cups all-purpose flour
- 1 tablespoon baking powder
- ¼ teaspoon salt
- 1 cup whole milk

FOR THE ICING:

- 1 stick (½ cup) unsalted butter, softened
- ¾ cup smooth peanut butter
- ½ cup cream cheese, softened
- 1½ teaspoons pure vanilla extract
- 2 cups powdered sugar
- 1 cup (about 24) dried banana chips (for garnish)

Preheat the oven to 350°F. Line two 12-cup muffin tins with paper liners and set aside.

MIX THE BATTER

Beat the eggs and sugars together in the bowl of a stand mixer fitted with the paddle attachment until light and fluffy, stopping the mixer twice during mixing to scrape down the paddle, bottom, and sides of the bowl. Add the oil in a slow, steady stream while beating on medium low speed. Add the vanilla and beat. Add the bananas and peanut butter, mix, scrape down the bowl, and beat.

Sift the flour, baking powder, and salt together into a separate bowl and set aside.

With the blender on low speed, alternately add the dry ingredients and the milk to the creamed mixture in three parts, beginning and ending with the dry ingredients. Blend just until the ingredients are fully incorporated.

BAKE THE CUPCAKES

Add batter into each cupcake liner until two-thirds full. Depending on the size of your cupcake pans, this recipe should make 1½ to 2 dozen cupcakes. Bake cupcakes for 15 to 20 minutes, or until a toothpick inserted in the center comes out clean.

MAKE THE ICING

Cream the butter, peanut butter, and the cream cheese together in the bowl of a stand mixer with the paddle on low speed. Beat until the mixture is smooth and creamy and no lumps remain. Add and combine the vanilla. Add the powdered sugar, 1 cup at a time, blending on low speed until fully incorporated. Scrape down the paddle, sides, and bottom of the bowl using a rubber spatula. Beat the mixture on medium speed until light and fluffy.

ICE THE CUPCAKES

When the cupcakes are completely cool, spread about 2 heaping tablespoons of the peanut butter icing on each cupcake, and garnish each one with a banana chip.

Peanut Butter & Banana Cupcakes will keep for several days covered at room temperature.

Jessica's Kitchen Wisdom

An ice cream scoop is the perfect implement for filling cupcake liners or tins with batter. One scoop should be just the right amount.

Peggy Hambright

Knoxville, Tennessee

BAKING A HAPPY LIFE

Eighteen years ago, Peggy Hambright was a graphic design student at the University of Tennessee in Knoxville when the Judybats, the band for which she played keyboard and fiddle, got signed. "It wasn't what we set out to do; we were just playing music, and it happened. It was this crazy whirlwind two years of touring and recording … I had no idea what I was doing. After we toured three albums, I began to rethink things. I missed being at home and having some semblance of a routine. I decided that I was going to quit the band and start some kind of business." And thus, Magpies Bakery was born.

Peggy began by baking cakes, pies, and desserts for local restaurants—first in a variety of local commercial kitchens, and then for five years in a makeshift bakery attached to her parents' house. Peggy's mother, who passed away in 2007, was an integral part of the start of Magpies. "My mother was my support. She did my dishes, the shopping, she was… I couldn't have done it without her. And I wouldn't have. We were kind of a team." Peggy also drew from the experience of watching her father, a self-employed piano technician, operate his business. In 2003, Magpies moved into a storefront in the Old City of Knoxville. "I started with a $2,000 loan from my dad (which I probably never paid back), and, until we purchased the building we are in now, I never got a loan or anything. I always put all the money back in the business." After a foray into serving lunches and a spread of desserts, she realized that "people just wanted the cakes and cupcakes." So she decided to focus on that. "I just got good with cakes. Letting go of pies was the hardest thing I had ever done." Peggy began focusing on weddings and cupcakes, and two years ago, she and her husband were able to purchase and renovate the large building in Knoxville where Magpies Cakes is now located.

" My one rule of business is to always try to do what you say you are going to do, and everything else will fall into place."

Peggy is a self-taught cake lady. Even though her mama was "the best cook in the world," she wasn't much of a baker. "But I learned to appreciate good food, being around her. When she would go to bridge club, she had that Betty Crocker Cookbook with the hardcover, and I would try to bake something that looked exactly like the picture. The first thing I made was the pumpkin pie." Even though she's built her business on cake, Peggy loves pie—she celebrates her birthday with that same pumpkin pie every year, and her favorite cake is the Key Lime Coconut Cake, "which, actually, involves pie."

Peggy says that she's learned a lot about herself and business in the 18 years since she started the bakery. "My one rule of business is to always try to do what you say you are going to do, and everything else will fall into place." Making people happy is a theme for Peggy, and

for her bakeshop; in fact, one of Magpies' slogans, borrowed from her friends at Yee-Haw Industries (a local letterpress printshop), is "Cupcakes Make People Happy." Peggy aims to make not just her customers happy, but her employees too. "I want people to be happy in my world. I want everybody to be happy doing what they are doing and I strive to pay a living wage. In the beginning, I spent a lot of time trying to create a happy environment for everybody rather than growing the business. But I reached a point where I realized that my job was to grow the business and make it successful, and the happiness would follow."

Peggy also, like many busy women, has worked to figure out how to run a successful business while being a happy person herself. "I have to make things. I get my creative ya-yas out by doing the wedding cakes and the sculpted cakes. I used to be mad about how busy I was, and how little sleep I had. But I've come to embrace my identity, instead of fighting it. I still play music, but I long to do more. I long to do more artwork, painting. But being a cake lady has come to define me. When I've thought before that I don't want to do this anymore, I realize that this is who I am to this community, and to everybody that I know. I know I've grown as a person more by the experience of owning this business, figuring out the balance with relationships and family. As a Southern woman, you want to please people, you just want people to be happy. But I've learned that it's *my* job to be happy, too."

German Chocolate Cake

German Chocolate Cake, one of the most popular of Southern cakes, is essentially a light buttermilk chocolate cake iced with a coconut and pecan cooked custard. Despite its name, German Chocolate Cake did not originate in Germany, but in Texas. While the recipe itself dates back to at least the 1920s, the name comes from the chocolate called for in the recipe popularized in the 1950s by the Baker's Chocolate Company: German's Sweet Chocolate. Peggy says, "This is one of those cakes you only want to make for very special people. And serve it in slivers—it's rich like heck."

PREP TIME: 15 minutes

BAKING TIME: 30 to 40 minutes

COOLING TIME: about 1 hour plus 30 minutes for icing to cool

DECORATING: 20 minutes (includes making the icing and filling the cake)

YOU WILL NEED
FOR THE CAKE:

- ½ cup boiling water
- 4 ounces sweetened baking chocolate
- 2 sticks (1 cup) butter, softened
- 2 cups sugar, divided
- 4 eggs, separated, at room temperature
- 2 teaspoons pure vanilla extract
- 2½ cups sifted cake flour
- 1 teaspoon baking soda
- ½ teaspoon salt
- 1 cup buttermilk, at room temperature

FOR THE ICING:

- 1 cup evaporated milk
- ¾ cup sugar
- 4 egg yolks
- 1 stick (½ cup) butter
- 2 teaspoons pure vanilla extract
- 1⅓ cups sweetened flaked coconut
- 1 cup pecans, chopped, and toasted

Preheat oven to 350°F.

PREPARE THE PANS

Spray the bottom and sides of three 9-inch round cake pans liberally with cooking spray. Place the pans on a sheet of parchment paper and trace three circles the same size as the bottoms of the pans. Cut the circles out and place in the bottoms of the greased pans.

MAKE THE BATTER

Begin by melting the chocolate: Pour the boiling water over the chocolate, and whisk until fully combined. Set aside and allow the chocolate to cool but not solidify.

In the bowl of a stand mixer fitted with the paddle attachment, beat the butter and 1½ cups of the sugar together until light and fluffy. Break up the egg yolks with a fork, and slowly add them into the butter and sugar mixture. Beat on medium speed until fully incorporated. Scrape the bowl down and add the cooled chocolate mixture. Mix on low speed until fully incorporated. Add the vanilla and scrape the bowl down again. Beat again until the mixture is smooth, light, and creamy.

Sift flour, baking soda, and salt together twice. Set aside.

With the mixer on low speed, add one-third of the flour mixture, then one-third of the buttermilk. Mix just until incorporated. Continue adding the buttermilk and flour mixture in thirds until it's all in there. Scrape the bowl well and gently mix again to make sure all the ingredients are incorporated.

In a clean, dry bowl of a stand mixer with a whisk, whip the egg whites on medium low until frothy. Increase the speed to medium high and gradually add the rest of the sugar until combined. Whisk the whites until stiff peaks form, but don't overbeat. Gently fold egg whites into the chocolate mixture, until just incorporated. Don't mix too much or the batter will deflate.

Divide the batter evenly among the three pans. Bake for 30 to 40 minutes, until the cake springs back when touched, the sides of the cake come away from the sides of the pan, and a toothpick inserted in the center of the cake comes out clean. Let the cakes cool completely in the pans on a rack.

MAKE THE ICING

Combine the evaporated milk, sugar, yolks, butter, and vanilla in a medium saucepan. Heat on medium low heat, stirring constantly with a whisk or wooden spoon for 12 to 15 minutes, until the mixture thickens. When the mixture has thickened, stir in the coconut and pecans. Let the mixture cool and store in the fridge until ready to use.

ASSEMBLE THE CAKE

When the cake layers are completely cool, trim off any uneven areas from the tops with a serrated knife. Invert the first layer onto a cake plate, parchment side up. Carefully peel the parchment off of the cake and throw it away. Spread one-third of the icing on the top surface of the cake with an offset spatula. Place the second cake layer on top of the first, remove the parchment paper, and spread another one-third of the icing—removing the parchment paper and spreading the icing. Repeat with the third layer. (Peggy doesn't ice the sides of her German Chocolate Cake, she says, "because it makes a mess.") Chill the cake for an hour or so until it sets up. Then slice into *thin* slices and serve, maybe with a little vanilla ice cream.

German Chocolate Cake can be kept at room temperature for several days or refrigerated for up to a week.

Peggy's Kitchen Wisdom

It's easier to put this cake together if you chill your layers in the fridge for an hour or so first. You can also wrap them and put them in the freezer for 20 to 30 minutes.

Make cupcakes from this recipe, too: Just fill two dozen cupcake pans with the batter and bake for 15 to 20 minutes.

Barbara Higgins & Sally Roberts

Asheville, North Carolina

FRIENDS ARE THE ANSWER

When I asked Barbara Higgins how long she's been best friends with Sally Roberts, she laughed and responded, "Well, almost forever!" When Barbara lost her first husband to cancer in 1965, Sally, a member of her church, brought her a cake. "She was so lovely, and we developed a really close friendship." Sally and Barbara have baked each other's birthday cakes every year since. Sally was there to help Barbara again in 2006, when her second husband died of Alzheimer's disease, and Barbara's friendship has helped lift Sally's spirits as she has dealt with recent medical concerns. "When you go through hardships, or you lose loved ones," says Barbara, "it attunes you to other people's hardships, and makes you search your mind and your spirit to ask yourself, 'now, what can I do to help that person?'"

The story of Barbara and Sally's friendship is the story of friendships between women everywhere: a story of giving and learning to receive the gifts of love that are offered to us by our friends, family, and loved ones. "Sally gets after me about me not accepting compliments, but I'm learning to be a grateful receiver of compliments. Giving and receiving—the whole thing is about love, and that's what we are all here for."

Both Barbara and Sally were born and raised in Asheville. Barbara worked as a home economics teacher for many years in the Asheville City Schools, and she and her dog, Pip, live in a house her husband built on the property her grandfather owned. As a child, she helped her family raise corn, vegetables, chickens, turkeys, and hogs and sold produce at the market in downtown Asheville. She remembers her grandmother baking pineapple upside-down cakes, prune cakes, and, of course, fresh coconut cake, which was a special treat at Christmastime.

Sally has lived her entire life in Asheville, as well. Friends, family, and church members have been enjoying her baking for decades. Her favorite cakes to bake are fresh apple cake, Mississippi mud cake, caramel cake, and pound cake. Sally says, "Barbara and I have been baking cakes for each other for 45 years. Barbara, do you remember that one cake I made for you about 20 years ago?—I put the wrong kind of flour in it, and put it in the oven? It exploded! I had cake everywhere. But I made it again and it turned out fine. And Barbara, she makes wonderful cakes for me! I love her fresh apple cake. Had Barbara and I not been doing this, I don't think either one of us would have had a birthday

Sally Roberts (left) and Barbara Higgins (right)

" There's no question that when you receive a home baked cake, you feel special. And if you are the one doing the baking, you feel special, too."

cake. No, we both grew up in families that didn't do birthday cakes. Then, I have two boys, and they're not going to bake me a birthday cake! But it's important—everybody's got to blow out a candle on their birthday!" Barbara adds, "There's no question that when you receive a home baked cake, you feel special. And if you are the one doing the baking, you feel special, too."

Sally said, "Barbara and I talk almost every day. We do every holiday together, with our families." When asked if her long-term friendships have helped her deal with hardships in her life, Barbara simply said, "Friends get you through. Friends are the answer. Friends...and dogs." Sally agreed: "Yes, friends. And definitely dogs."

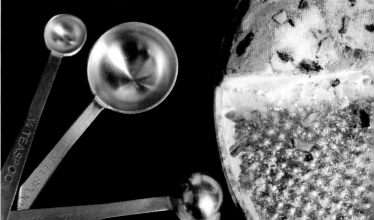

Mississippi Mud Cake

Mississippi Mud Cake—chocolate cake with a marshmallow and chocolate topping—is as well loved for its simplicity and ease of assembly as it is for its rich, moist flavor. This Southern favorite is so quick to make because once its simple topping is added, it's served in the pan it's baked in, warm out of the oven.

PREP TIME: 10 minutes
BAKING TIME: 30 to 35 minutes
DECORATING TIME: 10 minutes
COOLING TIME: about 2 hours

YOU WILL NEED:
FOR THE CAKE:

2 sticks (1 cup) butter, melted
½ cup cocoa powder
4 large eggs, at room temperature
2 cups sugar
¼ teaspoon salt
1½ cups all-purpose flour
1 teaspoon pure vanilla extract

FOR THE TOPPING:

1 bag (10½ ounces) miniature marshmallows
½ stick (¼ cup) butter
½ cup milk
½ cup cocoa powder
4 cups powdered sugar

Preheat the oven to 350°F.

PREPARE THE PAN

Spray a 9 x 13-inch rectangular cake pan lightly with vegetable oil spray.

MAKE THE BATTER

Using a rubber spatula or wooden spoon, add and mix all the cake ingredients together by hand until combined and no lumps remain, one by one in the order listed into a bowl.

BAKE THE CAKE

Gently scrape the batter into the pan. Place in the preheated oven, and bake for 30 to 35 minutes, or until a knife inserted into the center of the cake comes out clean.

MAKE THE TOPPING

When the cake comes out of the oven, distribute the marshmallows evenly over the surface of the warm cake. Set aside. Put the butter and milk in a large saucepan over medium heat and cook until the butter is melted and the mixture is beginning to simmer. Remove from the heat and whisk in the cocoa powder. The mixture will be slightly lumpy. Return the pan to medium heat and cook, whisking constantly, until smooth. Add the powdered sugar, 1 cup at a time, whisking between additions. Continue cooking, whisking, until the mixture comes to a simmer. Immediately pour the hot glaze over the marshmallows, covering them completely. Let stand until room temperature before cutting.

Mississippi Mud Cake can be kept covered in the refrigerator for up to a week.

Elyse Manning

New Orleans, Louisiana

CHAOS BAKING

Though she lives in New Orleans now, Elyse Manning is a legend in my community of Asheville, North Carolina. Elyse is known for her gifts as a musician, an artist, a loyal friend, and an impeccable hostess. But she first captured my heart with her particular form of baking magic—the rare ability to maneuver around any mishap or disaster that befalls her cake. Using your imagination to correct or cover up a mistake in baking is common, but few bakers can transform a bona fide disaster into a masterpiece the way Elyse can. I'll never forget the day that I wandered into her kitchen and watched her make a batch of what eventually became Mexican chocolate

cookies. As she added "a little of this and a little of that," it seemed at any given point that the mixture could just as easily become a chocolate chip cake, or perhaps a chocolate chess pie, rather than a cookie. I watched as she continued to taste the dough and recklessly splash unmeasured quantities of liquids, spices, and flours from unlabeled bottles and jars into her bowl. To me, her baking project seemed like a ship without a rudder—doomed to failure. When she batched out her cookies and confidently closed the oven doors, I had no idea that what lay in store for me 15 minutes later was the most tender, most flavorful, deeply chocolate, warmly spiced cookie that I have ever tasted. I still have no idea if she set out to make Mexican chocolate cookies or that's just what they became, but she has been my best friend and baking mentor ever since.

> " Making cakes has become part of my identity. People think of cakes when they think of me."

Born in Milwaukee, the daughter of a Puerto Rican mother and a Jewish father, Elyse was raised in Alabama and lived in Minnesota, North Carolina, and Tennessee before settling in New Orleans. Her jobs have almost always involved cooking or serving food, but her identity as a cake lady has more to do with family, friends, and community than her employment. "Making cakes has become part of my identity. People think of cakes when they think of me. If there's an event or celebration where cake needs to be made, I step up to do it, and people get excited about me doing it. And I enjoy it. I love making cake."

Trifle is a perfect example of Elyse's particular style of chaos baking. Once she was baking an elaborate hazelnut torte for a friend's birthday, and accidentally burned the layers. She'd planned on making small chocolates to garnish the cake, but accidentally used bittersweet chocolate instead of sweetened chocolate. The chocolate buttercream icing she had attempted to

make for the cake wouldn't hold up in the heat. Her cake, as she envisioned it, was a disaster. But Elyse did not give up. Instead, she changed her plan: She made a trifle. Cutting away the burnt parts of the cake layers, she soaked them in Amaretto. She whipped heavy cream into the broken buttercream icing and added the bittersweet chocolate. She garnished the trifle with toasted hazelnuts and crumbled bits of hazelnut cookies. Then, she put a birthday candle in that trifle, and she, the birthday girl, and all of the guests were happy.

Cake for a Mardi Gras Krewe

Elyse is a drummer with the brass marching band for the Mardi Gras Krewe of Eris. She describes the Krewe of Eris as "kind of a vagabond, punkish walking krewe, one of the hundreds of small walking groups that are initiated by handfuls of people that just want to costume and march around with their friends. The Krewe of Eris was started by some friends of mine in honor of Eris—the goddess of discord—a year before the storm. The first year I lived in New Orleans, our theme was The Appetites of Eris. I made a huge, wedding-style chocolate cake, and my friend Anais made golden apples out of marzipan, because there's this story about Eris not getting invited to a party with all the other gods and goddesses and getting revenge by throwing a golden apple into the crowd and saying, 'for the prettiest one.'" As the myth goes, Eris reveled in the chaos that ensued. Elyse's three-tiered chocolate Eris cake, complete with golden apples (and created with many baking mishaps and bold recoveries), was devoured by the krewe after the Mardi Gras parade.

Hair of the Dog
5 Buck$! 10am-5pm
BLOODY
MARY
...Call Now!... ....312 489 1842
—DELIVERY—

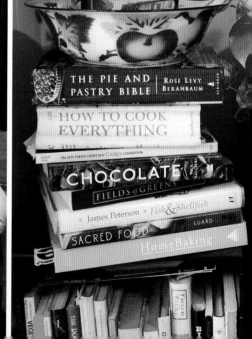

THE PIE AND PASTRY BIBLE | ROSE LEVY BERANBAUM

HOW TO COOK EVERYTHING

The SOUTHERN HERITAGE CAKES COOKBOOK

CHOCOLATE

FIELDS of GREENS

James Peterson • Fish&Shellfish

SACRED FOOD | LUARD

HomeBaking

Coconut Flan

While not technically a cake, flan—a simple, molded, custard-based dessert—is commonly found in Spanish and Latin American cuisines, and it also just happens to be gluten-free. Elyse says, "A lot of what I learned about cooking I learned from my grandmother, who made fantastic flan. It's our most cherished family recipe. Different people in my family have different ways of making it, but I try to stay true to the recipe she passed down."

PREP TIME: 25 to 30 minutes

BAKING TIME: 65 to 70 minutes

COOLING TIME: 1 hour plus at least 4 hours or overnight in the refrigerator

YOU WILL NEED
FOR THE CARAMEL:

1 cup sugar

⅓ cup water

FOR THE FLAN:

6 large eggs

1 8-ounce package of cream cheese, at room temperature

1 15-ounce can of cream of coconut (see Elyse's Kitchen Wisdom, at right)

½ teaspoon cinnamon

NOTE: Thinly-sliced limes add beautiful color and a citrus accompaniment to custardy flan.

Preheat the oven to 350°F.

MAKE THE CARAMEL

Combine the sugar and water in the bottom of a saucepan. Stir once with a spoon. Bring the sugar mixture to a boil over medium high heat. Turn the heat down to medium low. Use a pastry brush dipped in a bowl of water to brush down any sugar crystals that form on the side of the saucepan. Boil the caramel until it turns a deep golden brown, about 20 minutes.

MAKE THE CUSTARD

While the caramel is cooking, prepare the custard. Begin by blending the eggs well, adding them in one at a time, in a blender. Add the cream cheese and the cream of coconut to the blender and blend well. Add the cinnamon and blend.

LAYER THE FLAN

When the caramel turns a deep golden brown color, remove it from the heat. Immediately pour the caramel into a 1½ to 2 quart round glass casserole dish (use one with a lid), and carefully swirl it in the dish until the bottom and sides of the casserole are coated with the caramel; continue swirling the caramel around the dish as it cools to create an even layer on the sides and bottom. Let the caramel stand about 5 minutes to set. Pulse the custard briefly in the blender to reblend it and pour the custard mixture over the caramel and cover.

BAKE THE FLAN

Place the covered glass casserole inside a 10-inch (or larger) round pan. Fill this outer pan about two-thirds full with warm water. Place the flan, covered and in the water bath, in the 350°F oven. Set a timer for 45 minutes. Allow the flan to bake, covered, for 45 minutes, then remove the lid, and turn heat up to 375°F. Bake for an additional 20 to 25 minutes, or until the surface is slightly browned and the flan is mostly set but a little bit loose in the middle. Remove from the water bath and set aside to cool for 1 hour. Cover, and transfer to the refrigerator to chill.

When the flan is cooled, invert it by placing a plate upside down on top of the uncovered flan dish, and quickly flipping the flan onto the plate. Remove the casserole and let the caramel drizzle down around the plate. Slice and serve. The flan will keep for up to three days covered and refrigerated.

Elyse's Kitchen Wisdom

"The tricky part is the caramel. I tend to get impatient. If there's one thing I can stress, it's patience with the caramel. Don't be like me—take your time."

"Don't try to substitute coconut milk for the cream of coconut. Cream of coconut is thicker than coconut milk, and is more like a sweetened, condensed coconut milk. It has sugar in it, which is why you don't have to add any sugar to the recipe." Cream of coconut can usually be found with the alcoholic drink mixes (think piña coladas) or in the ethnic food sections of large grocery stores. Otherwise, try health food stores or Asian or Hispanic specialty food stores.

Trifle

Trifle, like many Southern dishes, was traditionally as much a strategy of thrift as a recipe. Made by layering scraps of other desserts, trifle is a flexible recipe that lends itself to experimentation, practicality, and the redemption of baking failures. The word *trifle* means something of little or no consequence, but a good trifle is actually a delicious and eye-catching dessert—it's usually served in a large clear glass pedestal bowl to show off its layered beauty. Because of its alcohol content, trifle is also known as Tipsy Cake in some parts of the South.

PREP TIME: 15 minutes
RESTING TIME: 1 hour and up to overnight

YOU WILL NEED

2 cups heavy whipping cream

½ cup sugar

4 heaping cups 1-inch cake cubes, any flavor (about 14 ounces)

¼ to ¾ cup sweet liqueur such as Kahlúa, Irish cream, Cointreau, or Chambord; or sweetened wine, such as cream sherry

2 to 3 cups of fresh fruit or toasted nuts

WHIP THE CREAM

Pour the cream into the bowl of a stand mixer. Add the sugar. With the whip attachment, beat the cream at high speed until stiff peaks form. Set aside.

ASSEMBLE THE TRIFLE

Crumble the cake cubes slightly and layer 2 cups of the cake cubes and crumbs in the bottom of a trifle bowl. Drizzle half of the liqueur over the cake. Spread half of the sweetened whipped cream over the cake layer. Spread half of the fruit or toasted nuts over the cream layer. Repeat with the remaining cake, liqueur, whipped cream, and fruit or toasted nuts. Refrigerate until serving and serve chilled. Trifle will keep for up to three days covered and refrigerated.

Trifle Ideas

Elyse describes trifle as having three main components:

1) a cakey layer
2) a creamy layer
3) a layer of interest

Here are some examples of ingredients that can be combined to make a tasty trifle:

1) chocolate hazelnut cake soaked in Kahlúa
2) heavy cream whipped with chocolate-hazelnut cream
3) toasted hazelnuts and crumbled hazelnut wafers

Or try this:

1) lemon cake soaked in limoncello
2) fresh whipped cream
3) fresh raspberries, crushed and sweetened with sugar

Or this:

1) vanilla cake soaked in banana liqueur
2) fresh pastry cream
3) fresh bananas

Use your imagination—save cake scraps and collect them in the freezer, and then use the thawed scraps, and fruits, nuts, and liquors available in your kitchen to create a new kind of lovely trifle!

Lois Mims

Pine Apple, Alabama

COOKING OUT THE BOOK

As I sat at the counter of the Pine Apple Grocery in Pine Apple, Alabama, James Huggins explained the origin of the town's name. "Back in earlier days, there was a stage coach route through the area, and a stopping place here—a watering hole for the horses with a pine tree and an apple tree, so they called it Pine Apple." Although the 2000 census listed Pine Apple as having 148 residents, a patron at the grocery (who was also a member of the City Council) guessed that the population had dwindled to about 70. Downtown Pine Apple, located at the corner of the Pineapple Highway and Banana Street, has a post office, a town hall, a library, some empty storefronts, and the Pine Apple Grocery, host of the annual Pine Apple Hunter Appreciation Day. It was through James at the grocery that I met the cake lady Lois Mims, who lives just down the street. Lois makes cakes for her friends and family, and, like many cake ladies, is often commissioned to bake cakes for sale. Lois has a reputation as a cook in her community. "They all call me Big Mama," she says. "Grown folk call me Big Mama. That's because I used to do a lot of cooking and feed a lot of people, and I didn't mind doing it. I enjoy feeding people. It makes me feel good."

Like many other cake ladies, Lois doesn't use written recipes; instead she relies on her memory, her intuition, and her experience to craft the perfect cake. "You talking about a recipe? I ain't got a recipe. I just put my stuff in there, take my head, and use it." Within minutes of meeting her, Lois proceeded to tell me how she makes several of her cakes, listing from memory the ingredients and methods for egg pie, cooked caramel icing, applesauce spice cake, yellow cake, lemon pie, coconut pie, and pineapple upside-down cake.

She recounted a baking story where she had to rely on intuition (and prayer) to get the right results: "One time I was making pies for some people, but I don't have money to buy piecrust, and I can't make them like my mama, so I said, 'Lord, help me to make these piecrusts for these people because I don't have no money.' So I got up and I rolled them piecrusts, and they came out right. They say the pies were nice, they were good."

"I enjoy feeding people. It makes me feel good."

Like many bakers, Lois credits her mother with teaching her to bake by feel rather than from recipes. She says, "There was a friend my mother used to cook for. My mother's name was Allie, and when I was a little girl, he'd say, 'Allie, she cook out the book!' And I always thought, I wonder what he's saying? After I thought about it when I was grown, I said, 'I know what he's saying! He's talking about how good my mama cooked, and she didn't have to use a book.'"

Applesauce Spice Cake

Lois had this delicious moist cake, which gets its warm, spicy flavors from cinnamon and clove, on the kitchen table when I visited her home. Lois doesn't typically measure her ingredients, but she was kind enough to estimate the amount of each ingredient that she uses.

PREP TIME: 15 minutes
BAKING TIME: 20 to 25 minutes
COOLING TIME: about 1 hour

YOU WILL NEED
FOR THE CAKE:

- 1 cup vegetable oil
- 4 large eggs
- ¾ cup sugar
- ¼ cup packed light brown sugar
- 2 cups self-rising flour, divided
- 1 heaping teaspoon cinnamon
- 1 heaping teaspoon ground clove
- 1 cup applesauce
- 1 cup whole shelled walnuts, coarsely chopped

FOR THE GLAZE:

- 3 tablespoons milk
- 1½ cups powdered sugar

Position a rack in the center of the oven and preheat the oven to 350°F.

PREPARE THE PANS

Spray two 9-inch round cake pans with cooking spray and set aside.

MIX THE BATTER

Combine the oil, eggs, and both types of sugar in the bowl of a stand mixer. Beat until light, fluffy, and fully creamed. Add 1 cup of self-rising flour, the cinnamon, and the clove, and beat until just combined. Add the applesauce, combine, and then add your remaining flour. Add walnuts and fold in with a spatula. Beat until just combined.

BAKE THE CAKE

Divide the batter evenly between the two cake pans. Place the cake layers in the oven, and bake for 20 to 25 minutes, or until a knife inserted in the center of the cake comes out clean and the sides of the cake pull away from the sides of the pan. Remove from the oven and cool in the pans on a rack for 5 minutes before inverting onto racks to cool completely.

MAKE THE GLAZE

In a separate bowl, combine the milk and the powdered sugar. Mix with a fork or whisk until no lumps of powdered sugar remain.

ASSEMBLE THE CAKE

When the layers are cool, place the first layer on a plate. Drizzle ¼ cup of the glaze over the first layer to cover the surface. Allow the glaze to drizzle down the sides a little. Place the next layer on top of the first and repeat with the remaining glaze. Applesauce spice cake can be kept at room temperature, covered, for up to a week.

Lois's Kitchen Wisdom

Lois told me, "Way back yonder we didn't have no mixer. When my mama used to fix the cake, we had to beat it 300 strokes every time."

Pineapple Upside-Down Cake

Lois stopped baking this cake for a few years, but then her children started to ask for it again. Lois bakes her pineapple upside-down cake in a well-seasoned 9-inch cast-iron skillet.

PREP TIME: 20 minutes

BAKING TIME: 40 to 45 minutes

COOLING TIME: 5 minutes prior to inverting, plus 1 hour before cutting

YOU WILL NEED
FOR THE TOPPING:
- ½ stick (¼ cup) butter
- 1 cup packed light brown sugar
- 1 15-ounce can of pineapple slices, drained and juice reserved
- 1 small jar of maraschino cherries (about 15), stemmed

FOR THE CAKE:
- 1 stick (½ cup) butter
- 2 cups self-rising flour
- 1½ cups sugar
- 2 large eggs, lightly beaten
- ¾ cup milk
- 2 tablespoons reserved pineapple juice from can

Position a rack in the center of the oven and preheat the oven to 375°F.

BEFORE YOU BEGIN

To melt the butter for the cake, place 1 stick of butter in a 9-inch cast-iron skillet and set it in the preheating oven until the butter is melted but not sizzling. Pour the melted butter into a heat-proof mixing bowl, and set aside. Allow the butter to cool, but not solidify.

MAKE THE TOPPING

Place the remaining ½ stick of butter in the skillet and place the skillet back in the oven, until the butter is melted but not sizzling. Remove the skillet from the oven, and add the brown sugar and stir until the sugar is dissolved; spread the brown sugar mixture into an even layer in the bottom of the skillet.

Place one pineapple ring in the center of the skillet on top of the brown sugar mixture. Arrange five pineapple rings in a circle around the center ring. Cut the remaining pineapple rings in half, and arrange the half-circles around the outside edge of the skillet, pressing them against the sides of the pan, cut ends up. Place a maraschino cherry in the center of each pineapple ring, and rest one cherry in each pineapple half-ring against the sides of the pan. Set aside.

Sift the flour and sugar together into the mixing bowl. Pour in the melted and cooled butter, eggs, milk, and pineapple juice. Stir with a wooden spoon until ingredients are just combined and few lumps remain. Gently pour the mixture over the fruit in the skillet. Scrape down the bowl with a spatula to be sure to get all of the batter out of the bowl and into the skillet. Use the spatula to evenly distribute the batter, cover all of the fruit, and level the batter's surface. Place the skillet on the center rack of the hot oven.

BAKE THE CAKE

Bake for 40 to 45 minutes, or until the top of the cake is a deep golden brown and a knife inserted into the center of the batter comes out clean. Remove the skillet from the oven and set it aside onto a heat-proof surface to cool for 5 minutes.

Run a knife around the outside edge of the cake to release any cake stuck to the pan. Place a heat-proof plate, inverted, over the skillet. With gloved hands, grasp both sides of the skillet and plate together, and invert the cake onto the plate. Remove the skillet. If any pieces of fruit have stuck to the skillet, quickly transfer them back onto the cake with a fork. The brown sugar glaze should drizzle slightly around the cake. Allow to cool, then serve immediately. Pineapple Upside-Down cake will keep for two or three days covered at room temperature, or for up to a week covered and refrigerated.

Pineapple Upside-Down History

The exact origins of the pineapple upside-down cake are something of a mystery. The technique of cooking a cake upside down by placing sugar and fruit in the bottom of a skillet with cake batter on top, and then flipping it to serve, is centuries old. But pineapple was not widely available in the United States until James Dole's Hawaiian Pineapple Company began canning the fruit in the early 1900s. By the 1920s, canned sliced pineapple was all the rage. In that same decade, a professor of horticulture at Oregon State University, Ernest H. Wiegand, invented a process for preserving maraschino cherries with brine instead of the traditional (and increasingly prohibited) maraschino liqueur. Once sliced canned pineapple and maraschino cherries were a pantry staple, it was only a short matter of time before someone (we don't know who) concocted a cake combining the two ingredients. By 1925, when the Hawaiian Pineapple Company held a recipe contest, 2,500 of the 60,000 entries (and the winner!) were for pineapple upside-down cake.

Michele Burton Oatis & Melissa Woods

New Orleans, Louisiana

THE CUPCAKE FAIRIES

Sisters Michele Burton Oatis and Melissa Woods, co-owners of The Cupcake Fairies, a home-based cake and cupcake business in the Gentilly neighborhood of New Orleans, never planned to open a bakery. Before the levees failed during Hurricane Katrina, their lives were very different, but once they returned to New Orleans after the storm, they realized that they, and their city, would never be the same. Michele says, "We lost everything. God, everything. Everything we worked hard for and

> "Baking is a science. It's not like cooking a pot of gumbo, where you can just do whatever."

invested in was just out on the street or waiting for us to open the door and throw it out. After that, after you've been through that kind of trauma, there's nothing else but your family." Michele not only lost her home and her family's business, but her career as a special needs teacher was destroyed, too, as the educational system in New Orleans collapsed.

While still grieving, Michele and Melissa set about building new livelihoods along with new homes. Michele and her husband rebuilt their home in Gentilly (the New Orleans neighborhood where they grew up), and the sisters helped to found the nonprofit New Orleans VideoVoices, an organization that puts video cameras in the hands of community members to help them create documentary films and "tell their stories and advocate for their needs and issues from their own point of view." Crafting brand-new lives in an almost-broken city, they turned to what they knew for comfort and fun: cooking and baking. They began baking cupcakes in Michele's kitchen for fund-raisers for the nonprofit, and, within weeks, family and friends were placing orders for their own celebrations. Michele explains, "We'd work during the day and bake at night. People would ask, how do you do this? We'd say, 'the little fairies help us.' And that's how the name Cupcake Fairies came about."

As demand for their cupcakes grew, Michele and Melissa began to develop more recipes. They realized quickly that "baking is a science. It's not like cooking a pot of gumbo, where you can just do whatever. You

Sisters Melissa (left) and Michele (right)

"Katrina has taught me, like the water flows, you've got to go with the flow. The current is going to take you, and it will lead you to where you need to be."

have to follow the science. So after a lot of trial and error, we've learned that we have to follow the rules of baking. But in that, you can be so creative. We've gotten so much positive feedback from our customers."

The sisters credit their father with teaching them to experiment in the kitchen. "He was always very passionate and creative about his cooking, and we learned to take risks from him." Building on their father's wisdom, Melissa and Michele began to experiment with vegan and sugar-free baking. They wanted to provide healthy but delicious desserts for

members of their community who were dealing with diabetes and other diseases. Melissa describes the Cupcake Fairies' food philosophy: "We're Southerners. You can't take a person who is born and raised here and say, 'because of your medical condition we need you to change everything,' and expect it to be successful, because food is so full of flavor here. So we want to make food that tastes good and that's going to fit into people's dietary needs."

And the community is responding: The Cupcake Fairies are delivering cupcakes and birthday cakes all over the city, and getting recognition in local television and print media. The response has been so great that the Cupcake Fairies are dreaming big: They bought the house next door to Michele's family's home, on a residential street in Gentilly, with plans to convert it into a commercial kitchen. That the markings of Katrina (those ubiquitous crosses spray-painted by search-and-rescue workers) still linger on the house that will soon be a bustling cupcake bakery is not lost on Michele and Melissa. Michele says, "We could have chosen to open a shop somewhere else. We could have stayed where we evacuated to in Tennessee. But we chose to be here, in New Orleans, in this Gentilly area. This house is a symbol of reclaiming New Orleans from Katrina. We need businesses in this neighborhood. We need jobs in this neighborhood. We want to support the local farmers, and get the economy going again."

While Michele and Melissa, and New Orleans itself, will never be the same, they're finding beauty in the transformations they have experienced since Katrina. Michele says, "Life just gives you everything you need. It took Katrina for me to let go of control. Katrina has taught me, like the water flows, you've got to go with the flow. The current is going to take you, and it will lead you to where you need to be. It took Katrina for me to learn that. I had to lose so much to gain so much." Melissa agrees: "We were always about community. And this work has brought me home to what I was meant to do."

Vegan Red Velvet Cupcakes

This vegan, low-fat variation of the classic Southern recipe gets its beautiful color from beets rather than red food coloring. The Cupcake Fairies are interested in offering healthier food to their community, and vegan baking is naturally low in cholesterol and saturated fats.

PREP TIME: 20 minutes (includes peeling, grating, and pureeing beets)

BAKING TIME: 25 minutes

COOLING TIME: 20 minutes

DECORATING TIME: 15 minutes

YOU WILL NEED
FOR THE CAKE:

  2 cups soy milk

  2 teaspoons apple cider vinegar

2½ cups all-purpose flour

  2 cups sugar

  ¼ cup natural cocoa powder

  1 teaspoon baking powder

  1 teaspoon baking soda

  1 teaspoon salt

  ½ cup vegetable oil

  2 tablespoons pure vanilla extract

  2 tablespoons unsweetened applesauce

  2 large red beets, about 12 ounces, peeled, shredded, and pureed (you should have about 2 cups of beet puree)

FOR THE ICING:

  1 cup vegan margarine (a nonhydrogenated brand is best), at room temperature

  1 cup vegan cream cheese, at room temperature

  2 tablespoons pure vanilla extract

  8 cups powdered sugar

Preheat the oven to 350°F. Line two 12-cup muffin tins with paper cupcake liners.

MIX THE BATTER

Combine the soymilk and the vinegar in a large mixing bowl, and set aside to curdle. In a separate bowl, sift the flour, sugar, cocoa powder, baking powder, baking soda, and salt. After the soymilk mixture has curdled, add the vegetable oil, vanilla, and applesauce to it, and stir. Pour the wet ingredients into the dry ingredients, and mix with a hand mixer until no lumps remain. Fold the pureed beets into the batter by hand with a rubber spatula until just combined.

BAKE THE CUPCAKES

Fill the lined muffin pans until each cup is three-fourths full of batter. Depending on the size of your cupcake pans, this recipe should make 2 to 2½ dozen cupcakes. Bake cupcakes for 25 minutes, or until a toothpick inserted in the center of a cupcake comes out clean. Set aside to cool. Once cool enough to handle, transfer the cupcakes to a rack, line six compartments of one of the pans with paper liners, fill, and bake the remaining batter.

MAKE THE ICING

Combine the vegan margarine and vegan cream cheese and beat until thoroughly mixed and creamy. Add vanilla and beat until combined. Add the powdered sugar, 2 cups at a time, and incorporate into the creamed mixture. Once all the sugar has been added, scrape down the bowl and beat for 2 minutes at medium speed.

ICE THE CUPCAKES

Place the cooled cupcakes on a serving tray.

METHOD I:

Using a spatula or a butter knife, spread 2 rounded tablespoons of icing onto the top of each cooled cupcake, swirling to cover the surface of the cupcake.

METHOD II:

Place an icing tip inside a pastry bag. Fill the pastry bag half full of icing. Squeezing from the top of the bag, force the icing through the tip onto the top of the cupcakes, swirling the icing around the top of each cupcake.

Serve at room temperature, and refrigerate any leftovers. Vegan Red Velvet Cupcakes will keep for up to four days, refrigerated.

Vegan Baking

A vegan diet includes no animal products, such as meat, dairy, eggs, or even honey. Some people are vegan because of health concerns, while others adopt a vegan lifestyle out of a concern for animals. Still others are vegan due to the reduced environmental impact of a plant-based diet. Many resources exist for vegan baking, most notably the excellent book *Vegan Cupcakes Take Over the World,* by Isa Chandra Moskowitz and Terry Hope Romero.

Helen "Tissy" Pass

Cordele, Georgia

LIVING HOME ECONOMICS

My great-aunt, Helen "Tissy" Pass, was born, raised, and has lived all of her life within the same two miles in Cordele, Georgia. The only exception is the years she spent as a student at the University of Georgia, where she studied home economics, and, as Aunt Tissy says, she's been living home economics ever since. The younger sister of my maternal grandmother, Aunt Tissy is known for her Italian cream cake. The delicious cake with its coconut and pecan icing is a popular request at family gatherings, and her recipe is the one that I use at Short Street Cakes.

Italian Cream Cake

stick oleo, ½ c Crisco
cup sugar 5 egg yolks
cups flour 1 Tea soda
cup buttermilk 1 Tea vanilla
small can coconut 1 c chopped nut
egg whites — Bake 350 - 25 m

pkg 8 oz cream cheese 1 tea vanilla
stick oleo pecans
box powdered sugar

Tissy says that she's been making her Italian cream cake for so long that she doesn't remember where she first came across the recipe, and indeed, there seems to be no definitive history of the cake, although we do know that Italian cream cakes became common in the South in the 1950s. Like many Southerners of her age, Tissy says her childhood memories of cake revolve more around undecorated fruitcakes and pound cakes than the traditional iced layer cakes we think of today as classic cakes.

The story of Southern cooking is, in many ways, a story of resourcefulness, using what is affordable and readily available to create decadent dishes from simple means.

While Cordele, Georgia, currently holds the title of "Watermelon Capital of the World," pecans remain a primary cash crop for the region. The fields and farms surrounding Cordele consist of mile after mile of pecan groves. It's no wonder that pecans play such an important role in Southern cuisine—the story of Southern cooking is, in many ways, a story of resourcefulness, using what is affordable and readily available to create decadent dishes from simple means. Tissy remembers that she used to harvest pecans and take them to the seed store to be cracked. She would then shell the pecans and put them away to use in her cakes and pies. Another cake recipe that Tissy passed along to me is her fig cake recipe—the one she uses when the figs come in and she "needs to use them up." Tissy's cakes are the result of a life of true home economics—a practical approach to baking that's closely tied to where we live and what we grow.

Italian Cream Cake

The Italian Cream Cake, like the German Chocolate Cake, has nothing to do with the country for which it is named. My best guess is that, because it's so laden with coconut and pecans, someone felt it needed a suitably exotic name to set it apart from an ordinary coconut or pecan cake. Etymology aside, the Italian Cream Cake is a Southern classic, and this recipe from my Great-Aunt Helen "Tissy" Pass is the best I've tasted.

PREP TIME: 25 minutes
BAKING TIME: about 25 minutes
COOLING TIME: 1½ hours
DECORATING TIME: 20 minutes

YOU WILL NEED
FOR THE CAKE:

- 2½ sticks (1¼ cups) unsalted butter, softened
- 3 cups sugar
- 7 large eggs, separated and at room temperature
- 1½ teaspoons pure vanilla extract
- 3 cups all-purpose flour
- 1½ teaspoons baking soda
- ¾ teaspoon salt
- 1½ cups buttermilk
- 1½ cups flaked coconut

FOR THE ICING:

- 2 packages (1 pound) cream cheese, softened
- 1 stick (½ cup) salted butter, softened
- 1 teaspoon pure vanilla extract
- 5 cups powdered sugar
- 2 cups of chopped pecans, toasted

Preheat the oven to 350°F.

PREPARE THE PANS

Spray the bottom and sides of three 9-inch round cake pans liberally with cooking spray. Place the pans on a sheet of parchment paper and trace three circles the same size as the bottoms of the pans. Cut the circles out and place in the bottoms of the greased pans.

MAKE THE BATTER

Beat the butter and sugar together in the bowl of a stand mixer fitted with the paddle attachment until light and fluffy, stopping the mixer twice during mixing to scrape down the paddle, bottom, and sides of the bowl. Add the egg yolks to the mixture, one at a time, stopping the mixer and scraping down the bowl after each addition. Beat the egg yolks into the creamed mixture for 5 minutes or until they are fully incorporated and the entire mixture is light in color and texture. Add the vanilla and mix until combined.

Sift the flour, baking soda, and salt together into a separate bowl and set aside.

With the blender on low speed, alternately add the dry ingredients and the buttermilk to the creamed mixture in three parts, beginning and ending with the dry ingredients. Scrape the bowl down between additions. Blend just until the ingredients are fully incorporated.

Using the whisk attachment on the stand mixer, whip the egg whites in a clean bowl until they hold a stiff peak. Using a rubber spatula, gently fold the whipped egg whites into the cake batter in three parts.

Fold in the coconut.

BAKE THE CAKE

Gently scrape the batter into the pans, dividing the batter evenly between the three pans. Place in the preheated oven, and bake for 22 to 26 minutes, or until a knife inserted into the center of the cake comes out clean and the sides of the cake have pulled away from the sides of the pan. Allow the cakes to cool for 20 minutes before removing the layers from the pans and setting on a wire rack to finish cooling.

MAKE THE ICING

Cream the cream cheese and butter together in the bowl of the stand mixer with the paddle, on low speed. Beat until the mixture is smooth and creamy and no lumps of butter remain. Add and combine the vanilla. Add the powdered sugar, 1 cup at a time, blending on low speed until fully incorporated. Using the rubber spatula, scrape down the paddle, sides, and bottom of the bowl. Beat the mixture on medium speed until light and fluffy. If the icing gets too soft to hold a peak, chill it briefly in the refrigerator, stirring often, until it thickens.

ASSEMBLE THE CAKE

When the cake layers are completely cool, trim any uneven areas from the top of the layers with a serrated knife to create a level surface on each. Invert the first layer onto a cake plate, parchment side up. Carefully peel the parchment off the cake and throw it away. Spread about 1½ cups of the cream cheese icing on the top surface of the cake with an offset spatula, pushing the icing over the edges of the layer and creating an even coat of icing. Place the second cake layer on top of the first and repeat the process—removing the parchment paper and spreading the icing. Repeat with the third layer, and then cover the sides with the icing.

Use your hand to press the toasted pecans into the side of the cake. Repeat all the way around the sides of the cake, creating an even coat of toasted pecan garnish.

Italian Cream Cake can be kept covered at room temperature for up to one week.

Fig Cake

This spice cake with figs and pecans can be baked in a bundt pan and glazed, or baked in a loaf pan and served as a quick bread. Fresh figs are usually in season from July through early autumn, depending on your location.

PREP TIME: 15 minutes
BAKING TIME: 1 hour
COOLING TIME: about 1½ hours
DECORATING TIME: 5 minutes

YOU WILL NEED
FOR THE CAKE:

- 3 large eggs, at room temperature
- 1½ cups sugar
- 1 cup vegetable oil
- 1 teaspoon pure vanilla extract
- 2 cups all-purpose flour
- 1 teaspoon baking soda
- 1 teaspoon salt
- 1 teaspoon nutmeg
- 1 teaspoon cinnamon
- 1 cup buttermilk
- 1 cup fresh whole figs, about 5, stemmed and diced
- 1 cup pecans, chopped

FOR THE GLAZE:

- 3 cups confectioner's sugar
- 3 tablespoons milk
- 1 tablespoon lemon juice

Preheat the oven to 325°F.

PREPARE THE PAN

Spray the inside walls of the bundt pan liberally with nonstick cooking spray.

MAKE THE BATTER

Beat the eggs and sugar together in the bowl of a stand mixer fitted with a paddle attachment until light and fluffy. While beating the mixture on low speed, add the vegetable oil in a slow, steady stream. Add the vanilla and beat until incorporated. Scrape down the bottom and sides of the bowl, and beat again until the mixture is smooth, light, and creamy. Sift the flour, baking soda, salt, nutmeg, and cinnamon together into a separate bowl and set aside.

With the mixer on low speed, alternately add the dry ingredients and the buttermilk to the creamed mixture in three parts, beginning and ending with the dry ingredients; scrape the bowl down with a rubber spatula between additions. Blend just until the ingredients are fully incorporated.

Add the figs and pecans to the batter and stir until just combined.

BAKE THE CAKE

Gently scrape the batter into the pan. Place in the preheated oven, and bake for 1 hour, or until a knife inserted into the center of the cake comes out clean and the sides of the cake have pulled away from the sides of the pan. Allow the cake to cool for 1½ hours, then invert the cake onto a plate and remove the pan.

MAKE THE GLAZE

Combine all the ingredients in a bowl, and whisk them together by hand until no lumps of sugar remain. When the cake is cool, pour the glaze over the top of the cake, allowing the glaze to drip down the sides of the cake.

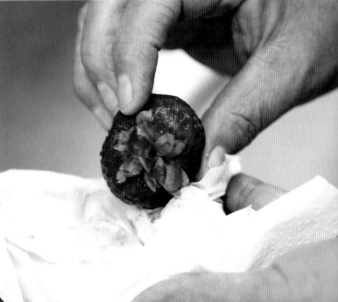

Matilda Reed

Cherokee, North Carolina

REED'S SOCO DINER

The first thing visitors notice upon entering Reed's Soco Diner in Cherokee, North Carolina, is the fresh strawberry cake. Along with such varieties as coconut cake and applesauce cake, the strawberry cake (with fluffy pink icing and sliced fresh strawberries on top) is prominently displayed under a glass dome on the counter. The strawberry cakes are well-known in this small mountain community as the labor of love of Matilda Reed, who co-owns Reed's Soco Diner with her sister, Iva Gentry.

Matilda and Iva, both members of the Eastern Band of Cherokee Indians, were two of nine children born and raised on a small farm on the Qualla Boundary, in the Smoky Mountains of Western North Carolina. The Qualla Boundary is the name of the 100-square-mile nation of the Eastern Band of Cherokee Indians. It's populated by the approximately 13,000 descendants of the survivors of the Trail of Tears who remained on tribal land or returned to the area. Matilda and Iva's mother taught them to bake. Growing up, they never had a store-bought cake; in their family, they made their own cakes. "My dad bought the self-rising flour, and we had lard from our hogs. We melted it down ourselves. And, of course, we raised chickens so we had eggs. We just learned baking from our mom. The recipe was always the same, but she would add different things to it. Sometimes we would spread sweet peaches on top, and sometimes huckleberries. We only got cake on Sundays or on our birthdays.

"Our favorite thing that our mom would make was the strawberry shortcake. When the strawberries were out, she would give us all buckets, and make us go out and collect the strawberries. And you couldn't eat any until you filled your bucket! She would make her strawberry shortcake out of a sweet biscuit dough, and she didn't use a cake pan. She would pinch off the biscuit dough for each layer, pat out the dough in a fry pan, and bake it in the woodstove. Just before we got to eat it, she would spoon her berries over the first layer, and then add the next layer, and then spoon it over again—it would be about five layers."

"Our favorite thing that our mom would make was the strawberry shortcake. When the strawberries were out, she would give us all buckets, and make us go out and collect strawberries. And you couldn't eat any until you filled your bucket."

While the Qualla Boundary is one of the most breathtakingly beautiful corners of the Appalachian Mountains, it is also one of the most impoverished, with the ten-year-old tribal casino being the region's primary employer. Matilda worked for seven years in the concessions at the casino before she and Iva were able to lease the diner and re-open the restaurant that had stood empty for years. Today, Reed's Soco Diner is famous for its Indian frybread and its meat-and-three homemade meals. Though the cakes she bakes for the diner are different from her mother's strawberry shortcake, they are just as treasured. The diner sells between two and three cakes by the slice per day, and Matilda loves that her customers always compliment their moistness and freshness. But the cakes aren't just popular because they are tasty—they also support a good cause. The money from any whole cakes sold funds the annual employee trip to Dollywood, Dolly Parton's theme park in Pigeon Forge, Tennessee.

Matilda and Iva are proud to own a gathering place for their community, proud to make cakes that are enjoyed by friends and neighbors, and proud of the Cherokee tribe's work toward cultural preservation and economic revival. Two of Matilda's grandchildren attend the Cherokee Language Academy—a school on the Qualla Boundary where classes are conducted solely in the Cherokee language. Matilda says, "My three littlest grandbabies have Indian names. Their names mean Goldfinch, Lost in the Woods, and Lucky Boy. And they are learning Cherokee, so I'm learning to speak Cherokee again. It makes me remember some of the words Mom said to me in Cherokee, and I can say them to my grandchildren. For special days or for their birthdays, I'll stack the cakes like my mama used to do. And I hope that one day, my grandkids will carry that on."

The Words Mom Said to Me: Cherokee Words for Common Cake Ingredients

ENGLISH	CHEROKEE PHONETICS	CHEROKEE	ENGLISH PHONETICS
egg	u-we-tsi	Ꭴꮻꮅ	ooh way jee
grain	u-dv-sv-u-ga-ta	Ꭴꮣꮢꭴꦗꮤ	ooh duh suh ooh gah tah
butter	go-tlv-nv-i	ꭶꮅꭴꭲ	go tluh nuh ee
milk	u-nv-di	Ꭴꮕꮧ	ooh nuh dee
sugar	ka-li-se-tsi	ꭷꮅꮪꮅ	kaw lee say jee
strawberry	a-nv	Ꭰꮕ	ah nuh

Strawberry Shortcake

This strawberry shortcake is an example of an Appalachian stack cake: simple layers piled high, sans icing, and with a sweet filling. This version uses stacks of sweet dough baked in an 8- or 9-inch cast-iron skillet.

PREP TIME: 15 minutes

BAKING TIME: 50 to 55 minutes

DECORATING TIME: 10 minutes (strawberries can macerate while layers are baking)

YOU WILL NEED
FOR THE SHORTCAKE:

- 2 cups self-rising flour, plus more for kneading and rolling
- ½ cup sugar
- ½ cup leaf lard, refrigerated (see Baking with Lard at right)
- 1 egg, gently beaten, at room temperature
  Scant ¼ cup milk, at room temperature

FOR THE FILLING:

- 6 cups fresh strawberries
- ½ cup sugar
  Put a well-seasoned 8- or 9-inch cast-iron skillet in the oven and preheat the oven to 425°F.

MAKE THE SHORTCAKE

Combine the flour and sugar in a mixing bowl. Cut in the cold lard with a pastry cutter until the mixture resembles coarse cornmeal. Add the egg and the milk, then stir the mixture with a wooden spoon until just combined. Knead the mixture gently in the bowl by hand just until it comes together. Transfer the dough to a floured work surface and knead until the dough is smooth and the consistency of piecrust—avoid over-handling the dough or it will become tough.

Divide the dough into five equal parts using a sharp knife. Flatten one of the five parts gently on a lightly floured surface with the heel of your palm. Use a lightly floured rolling pin to gently roll the dough into a thin, even circle that's slightly smaller than your cast-iron skillet.

Remove the hot skillet from the oven and carefully place the flattened dough in the bottom of the skillet, and gently pat it into a thin, even layer. Place the skillet in the preheated oven and bake until the edges of the dough begin to turn golden, about 10 minutes. While the first layer is baking, roll out the next layer. When the first layer is done, using a large flat spatula, remove it from the skillet, and place it on a rack to cool. Working quickly, press the second layer into the skillet and bake. Repeat with each of the layers.

MAKE THE FILLING

Wash the berries and slice off the green tops. Chop the berries finely and place in a bowl. Sprinkle the sugar over the berries and stir. Set aside for at least 15 minutes for the berries to release their juice.

STACK THE CAKE

Wait until just before serving to assemble the cake. (If you aren't assembling the cake right away, keep the layers wrapped in a tea towel at room temperature.) Place the first layer on a plate. Spoon enough of the berry mixture over the first layer to cover the surface. Allow the juices from the sweetened berries to drizzle down the sides a little. Place the next layer on top of the berries and top with more berries. Repeat with each layer, ending with the berries on top. Slice and serve immediately. Fresh whipped cream makes a great addition to this summer treat. This is a cake that's best eaten fresh.

Baking with Lard

Pig fat (lard), long a staple of Southern cooking, was once an economical alternative to butter and vegetable oil. Lard has been replaced by vegetable shortening in recent decades because of the decline of small-scale hog farming and concerns over lard's high concentration of saturated fats. Many bakers steer clear of lard, but others are rediscovering its superior results in pastries such as piecrusts and biscuit dough, while also recognizing that highly processed, hydrogenated vegetable shortening may pose its own health risks. If you don't want to use lard or you can't find a high-quality source of it (leaf lard is the highest quality), unsalted butter is a worthy substitute.

Pearl Teeter

Williamston, North Carolina

THE $1,200 CHOCOLATE CAKE

Pearl Teeter's grandson Ryan remembers the excitement he felt every year at Christmas when he knew he and his family would travel from Texas to the Eastern North Carolina town of Williamston to visit his grandmom and eat the ten-layer chocolate cake that was her specialty. "When we would get there, she'd have her cakes all laid out: red velvet, coconut, pineapple cake, Italian cream cake, mayonnaise cake, and, of course, the chocolate cake. The chocolate was always my favorite. I've always loved the thin layers—it just melts in your mouth."

Pearl learned to cook and bake as a young girl growing up on a farm outside of Williamston. "I started cooking when I was seven years old. My older sister slipped away and got married, and my mama, a few days before that, had fallen and skinned her leg badly and had to go to bed. Me and my oldest brother had to go in the kitchen. He helped me for a couple of days, but then

my daddy come in and says, 'I got to have him in the field.' So they left me by myself. My brothers would tease me about being so slow. But after I got married and looked back on it, I said, 'I was not slow! I had a lot to do!'

"I can remember Hoover days. That was a period of time that we bought very little from the grocery store. There was a lot of people going hungry, but we never did, 'cause we raised our stuff on the farm." She always baked cakes and pies for her family, but as she became older and started a family of her own, the cakes became her specialty. When her son opened a restaurant in Rocky Mount, she baked chocolate cakes every week for him to sell there—and her cakes were his biggest sellers. Pearl occasionally sells her cakes to friends and neighbors, too, but she enjoys donating cakes to community fund-raisers the most. Her cakes have become so renowned in her community that they routinely fetch hundreds of dollars each at church or community fund-raising auctions. One particular ten-layer cake that she donated to an American Cancer Society auction sold for $1,200!

"Her cooking is something that has always brought us together as a family, but the people in the community know her for her cakes."

As Pearl's grandson says, "On any given Sunday, siblings, cousins, aunts, and uncles will gather at her house to eat her wonderful cooking. It's not unusual for 15 people to pop in for lunch on Sunday. Her cakes have been there through all of our family gatherings. Her cooking is something that has always brought us together as a family, but the people in the community know her for her cakes."

Ten-Layer Chocolate Cake

The Ten-Layer Chocolate Cake appears in many incarnations throughout the South. In the Chesapeake Bay, it's called a Smith Island Cake; in New Orleans, a version named Doberge (pronounced DOUGH-bash) reigns supreme. The cake is not actually chocolate, but a yellow cake baked in many extremely thin layers and iced with chocolate icing. You'll need at least three 9-inch round cake pans, but gathering as many as you can get your hands on will make the baking process easier.

PREP TIME: 15 minutes plus baking time; it varies depending on the number of pans being used.

BAKING TIME: If you only have two 9-inch pans, it will take approximately 1 hour and 40 minutes, accounting for cooling time in between batches.

DECORATING TIME: 20 minutes

YOU WILL NEED
FOR THE CAKE:

6 large eggs, at room temperature

2 cups sugar

1 cup vegetable oil

1 tablespoon pure vanilla extract

4½ cups all-purpose flour

1 tablespoon baking powder

1 teaspoon salt

1¼ cups whole milk, at room temperature

FOR THE ICING:

2 sticks (1 cup) butter, softened

8 cups powdered sugar, divided

¾ cup cocoa powder

½ cup evaporated milk

1 tablespoon pure vanilla extract

NOTE: See Variation: Boiled Chocolate Icing (page 136) if you'd prefer a boiled icing.

Preheat the oven to 350°F.

PREPARE THE PANS

Spray as many 9-inch round cake pans as you have on hand (or can fit in your oven) liberally with cooking spray and line each with a 9-inch circle of parchment paper.

MAKE THE BATTER

In the bowl of a stand mixer fitted with the paddle attachment, mix the eggs and sugar together on medium speed until lightened and smooth. With the motor running on low, add the vegetable oil and vanilla and beat until well combined. In a large bowl, whisk together the flour, baking powder, and salt until combined. With the mixer motor running on low, add the dry ingredients and milk in three additions, alternating between the dry and wet but beginning and ending with the flour. Stop the mixer and scrape down the bowl and paddle between additions. Mix on low until very smooth.

BAKE THE CAKE

Pour a level ¾ cup of batter into each pan. Spread the batter on the bottom of the pan evenly to the edges, then tap the pan gently on a countertop to level the batter's surface. Place the pans in the preheated oven and bake until the edges are beginning to turn golden and release from the sides of the pan, about 10 minutes. Let the cakes cool in the pan for about 10 minutes before inverting and placing on a rack to cool completely. Re-spray each pan with cooking spray, line with parchment, and repeat until all 10 layers are baked.

MAKE THE ICING

Cream the butter and 4 cups of the sugar on low speed in the bowl of a stand mixer until thoroughly combined. Add the cocoa and blend, then add the evaporated milk and vanilla. Stop the mixer and scrape down the paddle, sides, and bottom of the bowl. Mix again until all the ingredients are incorporated, then gradually add the remaining powdered sugar, beating until smooth and creamy.

ASSEMBLE THE CAKE

Once all the cake layers are cooled, remove the parchment paper from each layer, and place one layer on a plate. Spread a level ⅓ cup of icing onto the top of the cake. Place another cake layer on top of the first, spread with ⅓ cup icing, and repeat until all 10 layers have been iced. Use the remaining icing to cover the sides of the cake.

Ten-Layer Chocolate Cake can be kept covered, at room temperature, for up to a week.

Variation: Boiled Chocolate Icing

Pearl's version is a modernized twist on the classic cooked chocolate icing: If you want a bit more of a challenge, you can make a boiled chocolate icing "the old way," by following this recipe.

YOU WILL NEED

5 cups of sugar

⅓ cup cocoa

1 stick (½ cup) butter, cut into pieces

1 15-ounce can evaporated milk

½ cup whole milk

2 teaspoons pure vanilla extract

Combine all the ingredients except the vanilla in a heavy-bottomed saucepan. Bring to a boil over medium heat, stirring frequently. Turn the heat down to medium low, and simmer the mixture for 10 minutes. Remove the icing from the heat and stir in the vanilla.

To assemble the cake using boiled icing, place a single cake layer on a plate, and spoon the icing over the first layer, making sure to cover the entire top surface and allowing the icing to drip down the sides. Center another cake layer on top of the iced layer, and repeat the icing process. Continue adding layers and icing them until all 10 layers are stacked. Use any remaining icing to coat the sides of the cake completely in the icing.

Pearl's Kitchen Wisdom

Pearl told me, "Back yonder I heard people say, 'You don't throw away your eggshells until your cake comes out, or else the cake will fall.'" To this day, Pearl leaves her empty eggshells out on the counter until her cake layers are safely baked and out of the oven.

METRIC CONVERSION CHART BY VOLUME (FOR LIQUIDS)

U.S.	Metric (milliliters/liters)
¼ teaspoon	1.25 mL
½ teaspoon	2.5 mL
1 teaspoon	5 mL
1 tablespoon	15 mL
¼ cup	60 mL
½ cup	120 mL
¾ cup	180 mL
1 cup	240 mL
2 cups (1 pint)	480 mL
4 cups (1 quart)	960 mL
4 quarts (1 gallon)	3.8 L

METRIC CONVERSION CHART BY WEIGHT (FOR DRY INGREDIENTS)

U.S.	Metric (grams/kilograms)
¼ teaspoon	1 g
½ teaspoon	2 g
1 teaspoon	5 g
1 tablespoon	15 g
16 ounces (1 pound)	450 g
2 pounds	900 g
3 pounds	1.4 kg
4 pounds	1.8 kg
5 pounds	2.3 kg
6 pounds	2.7 kg

COOKING MEASUREMENT EQUIVALENTS

3 teaspoons = 1 tablespoon

2 tablespoons = 1 fluid ounce

4 tablespoons = ¼ cup

5 tablespoons + 1 teaspoon = ⅓ cup

8 tablespoons = ½ cup

10 tablespoons + 2 teaspoons = ⅔ cup

12 tablespoons = ¾ cup

16 tablespoons = 1 cup

48 teaspoons = 1 cup

1 cup = 8 fluid ounces

2 cups = 1 pint

2 pints = 1 quart

4 quarts = 1 gallon

TEMPERATURE CONVERSION

Fahrenheit	Celsius
32°	0°
212°	100°
250°	121°
275°	135°
300°	149°
350°	177°
375°	191°
400°	204°
425°	218°

Acknowledgments

This book would not be possible without the guidance of Spirit and the love and support of so many people. My deepest and most sincere gratitude goes out first and foremost to my family. To my son, Jasper Macfarlane Rhoden, and my husband, Duncan Macfarlane: thank you for being my best friends, for sharing with me the source and ground of love and inspiration in this life, and for teaching me about the giving and receiving of unconditional love. To my mother and father, Sally and Jim Rhoden, thank you for your constant, steady guidance, and for setting an example of lives well-lived in integrity and in gratitude. To my brothers, Mitch and Jay Rhoden, and their families: I cannot express my gratitude to you for your constant encouragement and support throughout the process of writing this book, and indeed, all of life's many challenges and joys.

To the Short Street Cake Shop family, including Jenne, Nathanael, Shannon, Emilou, Lucianne, Adam, Hannah, and Anna: I thank you so deeply for understanding and sharing in this magic of cake with me, and for bringing your gifts of creativity and love to create something beautiful together, that none of us could do alone.

To my wonderful community of friends, customers, and fellow parents in Asheville: Thank you for believing in and supporting this work, and providing the fun and beauty to inspire me to keep doing it.

To Nicole McConville, Beth Sweet, Chris Bryant, Travis Medford, and all the talented and creative dreamers at Lark: Thank you for taking this idea and forming it into a thing of beauty. It has been such an incredible opportunity, and I feel so lucky!

Thanks to Lynne Harty for her delectable cake photography, and to Susan Patrice for capturing the beauty of Southern cake ladies.

To John T. Edge, Amy Evans Streeter, Angie Mosier, and Rat Head of the Southern Foodways Alliance: Thank you for your encouragement, support, and vision.

My gratitude also abounds for these friends, guides, healers, and helpers: Elyse Manning, Keri Frank, Lexi Ward, DK Brainard, Darcel Eddins, Sara Legatski, Ursula Gullow, Carrie-Welles Miller, Jaye Bartell, Mindy Gates, Braden Russell, David Hamilton, Rahn Broady, and Shannon O'Neill.

Most of all, I would like to thank the cake ladies: Betty Compton, Johnnie Gabriel, Lisa Goldstein, Jessica Grossman, Peggy Hambright, Barbara Higgins, Elyse Manning, Lois Mims, Mary Moon, Michele Burton Oatis, Helen "Tissy" Pass, Olga Perez, Sally Roberts, Matilda Reed, Dye Scott-Rhodan, Pearl Teeter, and Melissa Woods for so generously sharing their lives, recipes, and wisdom.

About the Author

Jodi Rhoden is a mother, writer, baker, and community food activist. She is the owner of Short Street Cakes, a popular bakery specializing in natural, scratch-made, traditional Southern cakes and cupcakes. Jodi serves as a member of the Southern Foodways Alliance and is a board member of the Bountiful Cities Project, a grass-roots urban agriculture organization. She lives in Asheville, North Carolina, with her family, and she chronicles her life as a baker, mom, and foodie at http://shortstreetcakes.blogspot.com/

Index

3 1901 04911 8930